D0919645

mama mia
ITALIAN COOKBOOK

The Home Book of Italian Cooking

MAMA MIA ITALIAN COOKBOOK

by Angela Catanzaro

Galahad Books • New York City

Library of Congress Catalog Card Number: 73-90677

ISBN 0-88365-216-1

Published by arrangement with
Liveright Publishing Corporation

PRINTED IN THE UNITED STATES OF AMERICA

Acknowledgments

TO MY MOTHER PAOLA, WHO BROUGHT THESE RECIPES WITH HER from her homeland.

To my sisters Philomena, Giovanina, and Maria, to my brother Vito, to Rev. John Raccanello, P.S.S.C., and to all my friends for their valuable assistance.

THE INTENTION OF EVERY OTHER PIECE OF PROSE MAY BE DIScussed and even mistrusted; but the purpose of a cookery book is one and unmistakable. Its object can conceivably be no other than to increase the happiness of mankind.

JOSEPH CONRAD

Introduction

MAMA MIA—"MY MOTHER"—AND TO MY MOTHER I GIVE CREDIT for this book. When she and my father came to this country from Sicily she was already famous for her cooking. She literally loved to prepare appetizing and delicious meals; and when my father died and she was left with five children, she turned to her skill with food as the best means of supporting her family. She cooked professionally for many years, catering for weddings, church suppers, and large social and business dinners. Mother's business was good because of her reputation as an excellent cook; but she was never too busy to teach her daughters the art of cooking. I look back even now with special delight to those hours spent with her in the kitchen; they were always enjoyable.

As the eldest I inherited the task of cooking for our large family, and then I really began to appreciate the value of my mother's precious training. When I worked as a Red Cross volunteer during the war, I served family dinners every Sunday to servicemen away from home. So many of the boys asked me for copies of the recipes I used, and so many complimented me on my Italian dishes, that I decided to publish the recipes my mother had given to me. This book is a tribute to Mama Mia—and I know that you who use it will share the joys and satisfaction my mother and I have felt in bringing to others the many delights of fine Italian meals.

Contents

mama mia
ITALIAN COOKBOOK

CHAPTER ONE

Characteristic Italian Foods

As you go through the recipes in this cook book, you will find listed many ingredients some of which may not be familiar to you—herbs, spices, cheeses, and other foods which do not usually appear in American cook books. These ingredients—fennel, oregano, mozzarella, provolone, prosciutto, capocollo, ceci, and so on—are largely responsible for giving Italian cooking its own special flavors. They are available in Italian grocery stores; and since Italian cooking has become so popular in the last few years, many of them are available in supermarkets and corner grocery stores. Since you undoubtedly have a spirit of adventure, you should be willing to make the slight extra effort involved in finding any unusual items; the recipes are well worth it. Here is a guide to those foods with which you may be unfamiliar, and which you will see listed time and again in the recipes in this book:

HERBS AND SPICES

Anise: Aromatic seeds with a slight licorice flavor. They may be bought in any grocery store. Anise seeds are used to flavor sauces, sweet rolls, and cookies; anise oil is used to flavor pastries. A liqueur made from the seeds is called anisette.

Basil: A sweet green leaf belonging to the mint family; slightly fragrant. May be bought dried in any grocery store. Used mainly to flavor tomato dishes and soups; also good with peas, squash, string beans, salads, meat pies, fish, and stews.

Bay leaf: Leaf of a shrub much like laurel, with an aromatic flavor which develops during cooking. May be bought dried in any grocery store. Used in stews, soups, boiled and sauted fish, and for pickling.

Capers: Pickled buds and young flowers of the caper plant. May be bought in any grocery store. Used as a salad garnish, and in sauces for meat and fish.

Garlic: The bulbous root of a plant which belongs to the lily family. The bulb is composed of many smaller sections called cloves. It may be bought dried in any grocery store. Used to flavor stews, meat dishes, sauces (especially tomato), and salad dressings.

Marjoram: A fragrant spicy leaf in the mint family. May be bought dried in any grocery store. Used in soups, meats, vegetables, and salads.

Mint: The aromatic leaves of the mint plant. May be bought dried anywhere, and during the summer, may be found fresh in most grocery stores. Used in stews, salads, meats (especially lamb), and with fish.

Oregano: The dried leaves of the wild marjoram plant. May be bought in most grocery stores and in all Italian food stores. Used to flavor soups, creamed fish dishes, sauces (especially tomato), pizzas, and vegetables.

Saffron: Orange-colored portion of the flower of the saffron plant. May be bought dried and powdered in gourmet food shops and in most Italian grocery stores. Used to flavor soups, sauces, and rice dishes; it contributes its color as well as flavor.

CHEESES

Mozzarella: A smooth, white, fresh, soft cheese, unsalted. May be bought now in most grocery stores. Usually used as a topping for meat and tomato dishes which are heated until cheese melts and browns and for pizza. May also be eaten plain.

Parmesan: Cured mild yellow cheese, available in Italian grocery stores. Also may be bought already grated in all grocery stores. Most often served grated with soups, meat dishes, pastas, and vegetables. Sometimes served melted over meat dishes and pastas.

Provolone: Mild light-yellow slicing cheese, usually molded into balls or long, slender sticks. May be bought in any Italian grocery store. Used for sandwiches, antipasto, and for eating plain.

Ricotta: A cheese much like cottage cheese; fresh, unsalted curds. May be bought in Italian stores, and in some supermarkets. Used in pie fillings, cookies, sandwiches, pastas, and salads.

Romano: Sharp, white, hard, cured cheese. May be bought in Italian stores. Usually served grated as a garnish, like Parmesan cheese.

FRUITS AND VEGETABLES

Ceci: Chick peas. May be bought fresh in Italian markets, or canned in any grocery store. Used as vegetable alone, or in soups and salads.

Fava beans: Green beans which resemble limas in shape and color. May be bought fresh in season (spring) in most Italian stores. Used like lima beans.

Fennel: Leafy stalks which resemble celery, but which have a licorice flavor. May be bought in most grocery stores, and in all Italian stores. Use it like celery, either fresh as an appetizer or antipasto, or cooked.

Pine Nuts: The nut-like seeds of one of the varieties of low pine trees. May be bought in Italian grocery stores. Be sure to buy them already shelled, as they are difficult to use otherwise. Used in cookies, meat dishes, and salads.

MEATS

Capocollo: Pork butt highly seasoned with ground red pepper. May be bought in Italian grocery stores. Used in antipasto and for stuffing for poultry.

Prosciutto: A spicy Italian ham. Available in Italian grocery stores and in some supermarkets. Used in antipasto, ground up in poultry and meat stuffings, and in egg dishes

PASTA

All pastas are essentially the same: a dried paste made from flour, water, and eggs. The paste is dried in various shapes, each of which has a name. Some shapes have special uses; the small, fine pastas are used in soups; the very large, tubular shapes are most often stuffed with meat or cheese, or covered with a sauce and baked. You will find most pastas in any grocery store; if you have any difficulty, all of them are available in Italian groceries. Most commercial brands of pasta have pictures of the shapes on the packages; just be sure that you do not buy an inappropriate kind for the method of preparation you want to use. Basic directions for cooking pastas of all kinds are given in Chapter 4.

Acini de pepe: Very tiny square or round pieces of pasta, used for soup.

Ditali: Tubular pasta about ½ in. long. Mostly used in minestrone.

Lasagne: Medium and wide noodles. Medium-sized lasagne are used in soups and with sauces, like spaghetti; wide ones are used in meat and cheese dishes.

Pastina: Very small rounds of pasta, used only in soup.

Rigatoni: Very large tubular pasta, cut in 3 in. lengths. Usually served stuffed with meat, covered with sauce, and baked.

Spaghettini: Long tubular pastas, a little thinner than regular spaghetti. Usually served like spaghetti, covered with sauce.

Tufoli: A very large tubular pasta, usually served stuffed and baked.

Vermicelli: Very thin spaghetti. Used in soups, either as it comes from the package, or broken into shorter lengths.

CHAPTER TWO

Antipasto

ANTIPASTO IS THE APPETIZER FOR AN ITALIAN MEAL. A GOOD antipasto, therefore, should be a combination of tidbits which will successfully whet the appetite for the coming meal; you should always keep the main course in mind as you choose the ingredients for the antipasto. Whatever you choose to serve should be arranged on a large platter so that the antipasto is as much of a delight to the eye as it is to the taste. The platter may be brought into the living room and the antipasto served there with small glasses of wine; or, if you prefer a more formal service, the antipasto may be passed at the dining room table as the first course of the meal.

An antipasto may be as simple or as elaborate as you wish to make it. Below are some ideas for combinations; but you should exercise your own imagination and ingenuity in offering to your guests colorful and appealing antipastos which will be only the start of exciting and tempting meals. *Salute!*

INGREDIENTS FOR ANTIPASTO COMBINATIONS

Anchovies: Serve plain, or garnish with lemon slices.

Capocollo: Serve thin slices or small strips.

Celery: Serve stalks, or celery curls made by icing small strips.

Cheese: Use mozzarella, provolone, or swiss cheese, cut in thin strips.

Eggs: Serve quartered hard-boiled eggs; or pickled eggs sliced thin.

Fennel: Serve stalks, or cut stalks in thin strips and ice.
Melon: Serve pieces of chilled honeydew or cantaloupe.
Olives: Serve green or black olives.
Prosciutto: Serve thin slices or strips; or, wrap pieces of prosciutto around small wedges of peeled, chilled melon, either cantaloupe or honeydew.
Salami: Serve thin slices or small strips.

ANCHOVY WITH TOMATOES

4 medium-sized tomatoes
1 2-oz. can anchovy fillets, with or without capers
Juice of 1 lemon
Pepper
Pinch of oregano (optional)

Wash and cut tomatoes into lengthwise wedges. Arrange on a small platter, and place 1 anchovy fillet on top of each tomato section. Combine oil from the canned anchovies with lemon juice, pepper, and oregano, and pour over tomatoes and anchovies. Serves 4.

PICKLED ARTICHOKES

15 small artichokes
2 qts. water
2 qts. cider vinegar
1 tablesp. whole mixed spices
1 tablesp. salt
2 tablesp. olive oil.

Wash artichokes. Remove large outside leaves around base, cut off stems, and trim 1½ in. from top of leaves. Boil water and add vinegar. Add artichokes. Liquid should cover artichokes; if it does not, add additional liquid, combining 1 part of water with 1 part of vinegar. Tie mixed spices in small bag, and add to pan. Add salt, cover, and cook over low flame 1 hour, until leaves separate easily from stem. Add oil, chill, and cut into eighths for antipasto.

CROSTINI

To prepare crostini, remove crust from day-old white bread. Slice into ¼ in. slices. Cut slices into 2 in. squares, or use a 2 in. cookie cutter. Brown squares in a little butter in frying pan, cooking on 1 *side only*. About 10 minutes before serving, spread the untoasted side with 1 of the following mixtures:

SPREADS FOR CROSTINI:

1. Soak 4 large salted anchovies for 2 hours in cold water. Wash well until all salt is washed out. Split in half, remove bones, and mash to a paste. Add lemon juice and blend well. 4 crostini.

2. Combine 1 2-oz. can anchovy fillets with capers, and 2 tablesp. grated Parmesan cheese, and mash to a paste. 6 crostini.

3. Combine 1 2-oz. can anchovies and 2 pitted green olives chopped fine, and blend well. 6 crostini.

4. Cut ⅛ lb. mozzarella cheese into thin slices, and then into 1 inch squares. Place a square of cheese on the untoasted side of crostini, and cover with an anchovy fillet. Broil 4 inches from fire for one minute, or until cheese is slightly brown. 8 crostini.

5. Chop 4 chicken livers into very small pieces, and saute with 1 tablesp. chopped parsley in butter for 2 minutes. Add 2 chopped anchovy fillets, and saute 1 minute longer. Season with salt, pepper, and ½ tablesp. lemon juice, and blend well. 8 crostini.

6. Chop 6 chicken livers fine. Saute with one minced scallion in butter over medium flame until lightly brown. Dissolve 1 tablesp. flour in 3 tablesp. stock or water, and add to livers. Cook 2 minutes longer. Do not allow livers to become too dry. Add more stock, if necessary. Season with salt, pepper, and ½ teasp. lemon juice, and blend well. 8 crostini.

7. Combine 1 3-oz. can tuna fish, 1 tablesp. lemon juice, and 2 tablesp. chopped parsley or basil. Blend well. 10 crostini.

EGGPLANT WITH ANCHOVY

MELENZANA CON ACCIUGHE

1 medium-sized eggplant
1 slice prosciutto, about ⅛th in. thick, chopped; or 3 anchovy fillets, chopped
1 clove garlic, chopped
2 tablesp. Romano cheese, cut into tiny pieces
1 cup olive oil

Select eggplant that is firm, with a glossy purple color. Wash the eggplant, but do not pare. Cut lengthwise into eighths, and make a slit about 1½ inches long on both sides of each slice. Mix the chopped prosciutto, garlic, and cut-up cheese, and stuff slits with this mixture. Heat oil in frying pan, and saute eggplant on all sides over medium heat until tender, about 15 minutes. It should be golden brown when done. Serve immediately on a hot platter. Serves 4.

LITTLE CUSHIONS

CUSCINETTI

6¼-in. slices stale white bread
3 thin slices prosciutto
3 thin slices mozzarella cheese
1 truffle, sliced (optional)
½ cup cold milk
½ cup bread crumbs or flour
1 egg, slightly beaten
1 cup salad oil

Remove crust from bread. Make a sandwich with 1 slice prosciutto, 1 slice cheese, and 1 slice truffle. Press together, cut each sandwich into 4 wedges, and fasten with toothpicks. Soak wedges in milk until moist; then roll in crumbs or flour, and dip in slightly beaten egg. Fry wedges in hot oil until golden brown on both sides, turning gently with a pancake turner. Serve very hot. Serves 3.

MARINATED FISH: *See p. 96.*

MUSHROOMS IN VINEGAR

FUNGHI AL SALAMOIA

½ lb. button mushrooms
1 tablesp. whole mixed spices
1 clove garlic
1½ cups wine or cider vinegar
1 teasp. salt

Wipe mushrooms well with a damp cloth. Heat vinegar until lukewarm. Put mushrooms in sterilized glass jar, add spices, garlic, warm vinegar, and salt, and stir thoroughly. Cover jar tightly, and set aside in a dry place for 2 days. Enough for 4.

One final word: Many of the salads which you will find in Chapter 11 may very easily be adapted for use as antipasto.

CHAPTER THREE

Soups

BASIC BEEF BROTH

BRODO DI MANZO

1 to 2 lbs. marrow bone, cracked
2 lbs. shin beef
3 sprigs parsley
1 carrot
1 small onion
1 ripe medium-sized tomato
1 celery stalk with leaves
Salt and pepper

Wash vegetables. Place all ingredients in a large kettle with enough cold water to cover, and bring slowly to a boil. Skim surface. Cover kettle and simmer for three hours, skimming when necessary. Strain broth through a colander and cool. Keep stock in covered glass jar in refrigerator until ready to use. Makes about 3½ qts.

BEEF SOUP

ZUPPA

1½ lbs. chuck beef or brisket
1 lb. beef soup bone with marrow
1 #2 can tomatoes
2 whole carrots
1 large onion, quartered
2 sprigs parsley
2 celery stalks with leaves, halved
Salt and pepper
½ lb. any soup pastina

Place meat and bone in a soup kettle, and cover with cold water. Bring slowly to a boil. Skim top with a spoon. Wash all vegetables and add to meat. Season with salt and pepper. Cover kettle, and cook slowly over low fire until meat is done, about 2 hours. Remove meat and vegetables from soup, and strain broth through a colander. Return soup to fire, add pastina, and cook slowly 8 to 12 minutes, until pastina is tender. Serve sprinkled with grated Parmesan cheese, if desired. The meat may be cut up and served in the soup; the vegetables may be pureed, if desired, and cooked in soup with pastina. The pastina may be cooked separately in 2 qts. boiling salted water, and added to soup after it is done; the soup will be thinner if the pastina is cooked separately.

VARIATIONS: If a spicy soup is desired, add ½ teasp. whole mixed spices in the last hour of cooking. Remove the spices when the pastina is cooked. If you like the flavor of bay leaf, add 1 when vegetables are added, and remove it about 1 hour before soup is done.

Or, 1 cup uncooked rice may be used in place of pastina. Cook it in the strained soup about 18 minutes, until a kernel crushes easily between thumb and finger.

TINY MEAT BALLS WITH SOUP

Prepare one recipe of beef soup. In the last hour of cooking prepare the meat balls:

1 slice day-old bread
1 lb. ground beef
2 eggs
2 tablesp. grated Romano cheese
1 teasp. chopped parsley
Salt and pepper

Soak bread in water 5 minutes, then squeeze dry with hands. Combine bread with remaining ingredients, and mix thoroughly. Shape meat into balls no larger than a filbert.

Strain soup. Add meat balls, 1 diced carrot, and 1 cup fresh shelled peas. Cook for 30 minutes. Add 1 cup any soup pastina, and cook 10 minutes longer. If desired, substitute ½ cup uncooked rice for pastina. Add rice with meat balls and vegetables, and cook only for 30 minutes.

QUICK BEEF STEAK SOUP

1½ lbs. round steak
1 carrot
1 fresh tomato
1 celery stalk with leaves
Salt and pepper
¼ lb. fine noodles or vermicelli

Put meat in soup kettle, cover with cold water, and bring slowly to a boil. Skim surface. Add washed vegetables and seasonings. Cover and simmer until meat is tender, about 30 minutes. Remove meat and vegetables from soup, add noodles, and cook for 12 minutes, stirring occasionally. Meat may be cut up and served in soup, or it may be eaten separately or used for sandwiches. Serve soup hot. Enough for 4. This broth is especially good for the sick.

CHICKEN SOUP

ZUPPA DI POLLO

1 plump fowl, about 4 to 5 lbs.
2 celery stalks with leaves, halved
2 sprigs parsley
2 scraped carrots
1 large ripe tomato (optional)
Salt and pepper

Have butcher clean chicken, but do not discard the feet. They add flavor to soup. Have butcher remove toes, then scald the feet and peel off the skin. Wash fowl thoroughly, place in a soup kettle, add skinned feet, and enough cold water to cover. Bring slowly to a boil. Skim surface. Add washed vegetables to pot, and seasonings. Cover tightly, and cook slowly until the fowl is tender, about 2½ hours. Strain broth, and serve as desired. Enough for 6.

VARIATIONS: Add 2 cups cooked rice to strained broth and heat until rice is thoroughly hot. Stir, and serve.

Or, cook ½ lb. pastina in 2 qts. boiling water, drain, add to strained broth, and heat thoroughly.

CHICK PEAS WITH RICE

RISO CON CECI

1 lb. dried chick peas
1 tablesp. chopped parsley
Salt and pepper
1 cup uncooked rice
2 tablesp. olive oil

Soak chick peas overnight. Drain, and cook in enough water to cover over high heat for 1 hour, adding more water to keep ceci covered. Reduce flame slightly, and continue cooking 1 hour. Check occasionally to see if any more water is necessary. Add parsley, seasonings, and washed uncooked rice. Continue cooking until peas and rice are tender, about 20 minutes more. Stir gently with a fork a few times. Turn off flame, add olive oil, and stir until well blended. Serve hot. Serves 6. If you want this thick soup to have some color, add 2 tablesp. tomato paste during the second hour of cooking.

CLAM SOUP

ZUPPA DI VONGOLI

12 little neck or cherry stone clams, in shells
2 tablesp. olive oil
½ cup water
1 clove garlic
1 #2 can tomatoes
1 teasp. minced parsley
Salt and pepper
2 slices of toast

Scrub clams with a brush, and rinse well to remove sand. Place in a large kettle with ½ cup water, and steam until shells open, about 15 minutes. Remove clams from shells, and strain juice. Set clam juice aside until ready to use.

Brown garlic in oil about 3 minutes. Add tomatoes, salt, pepper, and parsley. Simmer about 20 to 25 minutes, stirring occasionally. Add clam juice and clams. Continue cooking 1 minute longer. Pour over toast and serve immediately. Serves 2. Or, this soup may be used as an antipasto. Cut toast into points, and spoon soup over them. Serves 4.

FAVA WITH RICE

FAVA CON RISO

1 lb. fava beans
1 small onion, chopped
3 tablesp. olive oil
Salt and pepper
1 cup uncooked rice; or ½ lb. uncooked pasta

Soak favas overnight. Drain and remove shells. Put favas and chopped onion in enough cold water to cover, and bring to a boil. Cover pan, and simmer for 2 hours, adding water during cooking if necessary. Add washed rice or pasta, and cook until rice and favas are tender, stirring occasionally. Add oil, salt, and pepper, and serve immediately. Serves 4.
NOTE: Favas are sometimes called horsebeans. They can be purchased in any Italian grocery store. Fresh green lima beans are similar to favas, although the fava is somewhat rounder.

MINESTRONE

Minestrone is a thick soup, mostly made from fresh vegetables. There are a great many varieties of minestrone. It seems as though practically every Italian village, city, and town has its own way to prepare this basic Italian dish. Furthermore, Italian housewives are apt to vary their minestrone according to the vegetables that are in season. Here are some of the most popular kinds of minestrone.

CALAMONICIA MINESTRONE

1 cup dried kidney or navy beans
3 tablesp. olive oil
1 clove garlic, chopped
1 large onion, chopped
1 cup canned tomatoes
1 cup shelled peas
1 cup shelled fava beans
1 tablesp. chopped parsley
1 celery stalk, chopped
1 carrot, diced
1 cup raw potatoes, diced
2 qts. soup stock
Salt and pepper
½ lb. spaghetti cut into ½ in. pieces; or, 1 cup uncooked rice

Soak dried beans overnight. Drain. Pour oil into soup pot, add garlic, onion, and vegetables. Cover pot and simmer for 15 minutes, stirring often. Add soaked beans, soup stock, and seasonings. Cover and simmer until beans are tender, about 1¼ hours. Add spaghetti or rice, and simmer 15 minutes longer. Stir occasionally. Serve hot with grated Parmesan cheese. Serves 6.

CARMELLA'S MINESTRONE

1 cup dried navy beans
1 lb. pork shoulder, cut into 1½ in. pieces
1 lb. ham, cut into 1½ in. pieces
1 small onion, chopped
1 clove garlic, chopped (optional)
1 cup uncooked rice
1 small head of young cabbage, cut into eighths
¼ cup grated Parmesan cheese

Soak beans overnight. Drain. Place beans in soup kettle, add water to cover, pork meat, ham, onion, and garlic. Cover and cook slowly over low flame for 1½ hours. Add a little hot water if soup gets too thick. Wash rice, and add to soup. Cook 20 minutes longer. While rice is cooking in soup, cook cabbage in a separate pan of boiling salted water for 5 minutes. Drain, and add to minestrone. Cook 10 minutes longer. Serve hot, sprinkled with grated Parmesan cheese. Serves 6.

NOTE: This is a very thick minestrone. Since ham has a tendency to be salty, it is usually not necessary to add salt.

CHOPPED MEAT MINESTRONE

MINESTRONE DI CARNE

1 lb. ground beef
3 small onions, chopped
1 #2 can tomatoes
3 celery stalks with leaves, chopped
¼ cup fresh lima beans, shelled
¼ cup fresh string beans, cut into 1 in. pieces
1 cup fresh peas, shelled
¼ cup carrots, diced
Salt and pepper

Brown chopped meat with onion in soup pot about 10 minutes, stirring often. Add tomatoes, and simmer about 5 minutes. Add vegetables. Continue simmering for 5 minutes. Add cold water to cover, and seasonings. Cover pan, and simmer until vegetables are tender, about 40 minutes. Serve hot. Serves 6. This tasty and nourishing soup is excellent for children.

NOTE: If desired, omit lima beans, string beans, peas, and carrots, and use a box of frozen mixed vegetables instead. Add vegetables to boiling meat stock and cook until tender.

GENOAN MINESTRONE

MINESTRONE ALLA GENOVESE

3 tablesp. olive oil
2 onions, minced
2 qts. meat stock
3 celery stalks with leaves, diced
¼ lb. spinach, chopped
1 tablesp. minced parsley
¼ cup carrots, chopped
1 cup green beans, cut in 1 in. pieces
1 cup fresh shelled peas
1 cup canned peas
2 tablesp. tomato paste
Salt and pepper
1 cup elbow macaroni
1 cup grated Parmesan or Romano cheese

Saute onions in oil until light yellow and soft. Add soup stock, and bring to a boil. Add vegetables, tomato paste, and seasonings. Cover pot and simmer 20 minutes, adding a little more stock if soup gets too thick. Add elbow macaroni and continue cooking until vegetables and macaroni are tender, about 15 to 20 minutes. Stir occasionally. Serve hot, and sprinkle generously with cheese. Serves 4.

MEATLESS MINESTRONE

MINESTRONE SENZA CARNE

2 tablesp. olive oil
1 large onion, chopped
1 cup escarole, cut into 1 in. pieces
1 cup zucchini, unpeeled, and diced
2 zucchini leaves and 1 zucchini flower, chopped
1 celery stalk with leaves, chopped
1 cup string beans, cut in 1 in. pieces
1 knob kohlrabi, peeled and diced
Salt and pepper
½ lb. ditali or shell macaroni

Brown onion in oil for 3 minutes, add 3 qts. water, and bring to a boil. Add vegetables and seasonings. Cover and cook for 15 minutes over a medium flame. Add ditali and cook until vegetables and ditali are tender, about 20 minutes longer. Serve hot sprinkled with grated Parmesan cheese.

PEASANT MINESTRONE

MINESTRONE RUSTICA

½ small cabbage
2 carrots
1 large onion
2 white turnips
2 stalks swiss chard
¼ head chicory
2 tablesp. parsley
½ lb. fresh broad beans (optional)
½ lb. spareribs
Salt and pepper
2 qts. boiling water
1 lb. sweet Italian sausage, in links
1 cup grated cheese

Wash and chop all vegetables except broad beans. Put vegetables in large soup pot with spareribs, add boiling water, cover pan tightly, and cook over low flame 1½ hours. Add sausage and cook another 20 to 30 minutes, until vegetables are tender and sausage is done. Serve very hot with grated cheese. Serves 4.

RICE MINESTRONE

RISO MINESTRONE

1 small onion, chopped; or, 1 clove garlic, chopped fine
3 tablesp. olive oil
2 cups canned tomatoes
1 qt. soup stock
½ cup chopped carrots
1 cup fresh shelled peas, or fresh shelled lima beans
½ cup shredded cabbage
6 tablesp. uncooked rice
Salt and pepper

Brown onion in oil in soup pot until light brown. Add tomatoes and simmer 5 minutes, stirring occasionally. Add stock, and bring to a boil. Add carrots, remaining vegetables, rice, and seasonings to boiling stock. Cover and simmer until vegetables are tender, about 1 hour. Stir frequently. Serve very hot sprinkled with grated cheese. Enough for 4.

RICE AND PEA SOUP

MINESTRA DI RISO E PISELLI

⅓ cup butter or olive oil
1 slice bacon, chopped
1 slice prosciutto, chopped (optional)
1 small onion, minced
1 tablesp. parsley, minced
2 lbs. fresh green peas
1 qt. soup stock or water
½ cup uncooked rice
Salt and pepper
3 tablesp. grated Parmesan cheese

Saute onion, bacon, ham, and parsley in oil or butter until light brown. Add peas and cook 5 minutes, stirring frequently.

Add liquid, and bring to boil. Add washed rice, seasonings, and cheese. Cook over medium heat until rice crushes easily between fingers. Serve very hot. Serves 4.

ROMAN BROTH WITH EGG DROPS

STRACIATELLA ALLA ROMANA

2½ lbs. veal knuckles
1 lb. short ribs of beef, or chuck
1 celery stalk with leaves, diced
½ cup diced onion
½ teasp. marjoram
Salt and pepper
4 eggs
2½ tablesp. grated Parmesan cheese
1 tablesp. chopped parsley

Place meat with 3 qts. cold water in kettle, cover, and bring to a boil. Skim surface, and add celery, onion, marjoram, salt, and pepper. Cover and cook slowly over low flame until meat is very tender. Skim occasionally. Strain 7 cups broth into sauce pan, and keep hot while you prepare egg drops.

Beat eggs, cheese, and parsley together very well. Bring the 7 cups of broth to the boiling point, and gradually pour egg mixture into it, stirring constantly with a fork or wooden spoon to prevent lumping. Simmer until egg drops are cooked, about 5 minutes. Serve hot. Serves 6.

NOTE: Use remaining broth for stock. Use meat in sandwiches or salads.

SOUP PALERMO STYLE

MINESTRA ALLA PALERMITANA

½ lb. dried kidney beans or lentils
½ lb. dried chestnuts, shelled
1 celery stalk, diced
1 small onion, chopped
1 cup uncooked rice
4 tablesp. olive oil
Salt and pepper

Soak beans and chestnuts overnight. Drain. Place them in a large kettle, add 3 qts. cold water, celery, and onion, and simmer until beans and chestnuts are soft, about 1½ hours. Add washed rice, oil, and seasonings. Cook until rice is tender, about 20 minutes more, stirring constantly with a wooden spoon to prevent sticking. If necessary, add more water. Serve immediately. Serves 4.

SEA PERCH BROTH

BRODO DI PESCE ROSSO

1 sea perch, about 1½ lbs.
4 tablesp. olive oil
1 small onion, or 1 clove garlic, chopped
¼ cup canned tomatoes (optional)
¼ cup chopped parsley
2 qts. water
Salt and pepper
Pinch of saffron (optional)
1 cup fine noodles or vermicelli, cut into 1 in. pieces

Have fish dealer clean fish, but leave head and tail on. Brown onion in oil over medium fire until soft. Add tomatoes and parsley. Cook for 1 minute longer, mashing tomatoes with a fork. Add water, seasonings, and bring to a boil. Add fish and saffron. Cook over low fire until fish is tender, about 15 minutes. Remove from flame, and take fish out of broth with a pancake turner or slotted spoon. Remove back bone and small bones from fish, and break meat into small pieces. Strain broth through a colander. Add small pieces of fish to strained broth, return to fire, and bring to a boil. Add noodles, and cook over medium fire 10 minutes, stirring occasionally. Correct seasoning, and serve piping hot, sprinkled with grated Parmesan cheese. Serves 4.

NOTE: Sea perch are also called bright eye, rose fish, and red fish.

TUSCANY BEANS

FAGIOLI ALLA TOSCANA

1 lb. dried navy beans
4 qts. water
1 celery stalk with leaves, chopped
1 carrot, chopped
¼ lb. salt pork, ham, or ham rind, chopped
2 tablesp. tomato paste
Salt and pepper

Soak beans overnight. Drain. Place beans in water with celery, carrot, chopped pork or ham, tomato paste, and seasonings. Cover pot and cook over low flame until beans press easily between fingers, about 2½ to 3 hours. Soup should be thick. Serve very hot. Serves 6.

Accompaniments for Soups

CROUTONS

CROSTINI

3 eggs, separated
2 tablesp. melted butter
3 tablesp. sifted flour

Beat egg yolks and melted butter together. Add flour and blend well. Beat egg whites until frothy, and fold into yolk mixture. Pour into a 9 in. pan lined with waxed paper. Bake in moderate oven 350° for 10 or 15 minutes, until golden brown. Cool and cut into 1 in. cubes. Place croutons in soup bowl, and pour hot soup over them. Sprinkle with grated cheese, and serve immediately.

GARLIC CROUTONS

CROSTINI DI AGLIO

1 long loaf Italian bread
½ cup olive oil
2 cloves garlic, crushed
1 slice mozzarella cheese ¼ in. thick for each slice of bread (10 or 12)

Cut bread into 1 in. slices, and toast in moderate oven 350° until dried out, about 5 minutes. Heat oil in frying pan, add the crushed garlic and saute for a few seconds, but do not brown. Take the bread out of the oven and dip the slices in the oil. Place a slice of cheese over toast, and return to oven for 5 minutes, until cheese melts. Serve piping hot with soup, salads, beer, wine, or as an antipasto. Serves 10.

SOUP OF PARADISE

PASSATELLI

4 cups bread crumbs
1 cup grated Parmesan cheese
¼ cup flour
1 teasp. cinnamon
Pinch of ground allspice or nutmeg
Grated rind of 1 lemon
4 to 6 eggs
Chicken soup

Combine all ingredients except eggs and soup, and mix well. Add 4 eggs; if they are not enough to make a firm mixture, add 1 or 2 more. If mixture becomes very moist, add more bread crumbs. You should have a firm, not too wet, dough. Pinch off pieces of dough the size of a walnut, and roll them between palms of hands to the size and thickness of a pencil. Drop them in clear boiling chicken broth, and cook over medium flame 20 minutes. Stir gently during boiling. Serve hot. Serves 6.

VEAL DUMPLINGS

GNOCCHI DI VITELLO

2 slices white bread
½ cup milk
½ lb. veal steak
⅛ lb. suet, or ham
1 egg
1 egg yolk
3 tablesp. grated Romano cheese
Pinch of nutmeg
Salt and pepper
1 tablesp. melted butter

Soak bread in milk, and squeeze dry. Put meat and suet or ham through a food chopper, using a fine blade. Combine meat, bread, and remaining ingredients. (Caution: if you use ham instead of suet, use very little salt.) Mix thoroughly, and refrigerate for about 2 hours, until meat is firm and easy to handle. Take tablespoonfuls of the meat and shape them into balls the size of a walnut. Place the shaped gnocchi on a spoon and slide them gently one at a time into boiling chicken or meat soup. Cover pot and cook over a low fire 12 to 15 minutes. Serve very hot in the same soup. Sprinkle with grated Parmesan cheese, if desired. Serves 4.

LITTLE HATS: *See p. 45.*

CHICKEN DUMPLINGS: *See p. 51.*

CHAPTER FOUR

Pasta

HINTS FOR COOKING

Pasta IS A GENERAL TERM FOR PASTES MADE FROM WHEAT FLOUR, which are rolled very thin and dried into the various familiar forms of spaghetti, noodles, and macaroni. Pasta may be served as a main dish, stuffed with meat or cheese, and covered with a variety of succulent sauces; or it may be served as a side dish or vegetable, in which case it is usually not stuffed, but merely served with a sauce. Pasta is usually considered easy to prepare; but there is one trick you should know which will add to its tenderness. The amount of water used is the important thing. Be sure to use enough—never less than 5 quarts of water salted with 2 tablesp. of salt per pound of pasta. Let water boil briskly for 2 minutes before adding pasta. If short lengths of spaghetti or macaroni are desired, break the strands before you add them to the water.

Be sure not to overcook pasta so that it becomes mushy. It should be slightly chewy (*al dente*). Macaroni usually takes longer to cook than spaghetti, depending on its size and thickness. A general guide to cooking time is:

Spaghetti: 15 to 20 minutes
Spaghettini: 10 to 12 minutes
Macaroni: 15 to 20 minutes
Noodles: 10 to 20 minutes

Cooking time varies somewhat with different brands. The best thing to do is to cook it according to your own taste. Pasta may be tested for doneness by putting some in a dish and breaking it with a fork. If it cuts easily, it has cooked enough.

Before draining cooked pasta, run cold water into the boiling pot just long enough to stop the boiling, but not long enough to cool the pasta. This process removes some of the starch, but will not spoil the flavor. Drain pasta in colander, and serve with any desired sauce.

PASTA WITH NAVY BEANS

PASTA CON FAGIOLI

1 lb. dried navy beans
2 celery stalks, diced
1 large onion, chopped
5 tablesp. olive oil
Salt and pepper
½ lb. ditali, tubetini, or spaghetti broken into 1 in. pieces

Soak beans overnight in cold water. Drain, cover with fresh cold water, and bring to a boil. Add all ingredients except pasta, cover, and simmer over low fire until beans crush easily between fingers, about 2½ hours. Add pasta and simmer until it is tender, about 10 minutes more. Stir occasionally. Serve hot. Serves 6.

VARIATIONS: Add 1 cup canned tomatoes or fresh peeled tomatoes to ingredients. Dried kidney beans, chick peas, or dried lima beans may be substituted for navy beans, if desired.

PASTA WITH RICOTTA SAUCE

SALSA DI RICOTTA CON PASTA

1 small onion
4 tablesp. olive oil
1 lb. ricotta
1 can tomato puree
½ can tomato paste
1½ cups water
Salt and pepper
1 lb. short macaroni or spaghetti
4 tablesp. grated Romano cheese

Brown onion in oil. Add ricotta, tomato puree, tomato paste, and water. Mix until ricotta is in small pieces. Season with salt and pepper, and cook slowly over a low flame for 1 hour, stirring occasionally. While sauce is cooking, prepare pasta. Pour sauce over cooked macaroni, sprinkle with cheese, and serve immediately. Serves 4 to 6.

HOME MADE NOODLES

LASAGNE

3 cups sifted flour	*3 tablesp. lukewarm water*
3 eggs	*½ teasp. salt*

Sift flour on to a large board or table top. Make a well in center of flour, and put eggs, water, and salt into it. Knead thoroughly for 1 minute, until dough is stiff and elastic. Do not overknead, or dough will be tough. Add more flour if dough is thin, or a few drops of water if dough seems dry.

Divide dough in thirds. Roll each part paper thin on a slightly floured board or table top. Sprinkle sheets of rolled dough with a very little flour, and let them stand until they turn deep gold in color, about 15 minutes. Do not allow them to get very dry. After sheets have dried 15 minutes, roll each one up like a jelly roll. With a sharp knife cut the rolls into ¼ to ½ in. strips. Take each strip and shake it out to its full length. Place strips on a dry floured cloth ½ in. apart, and dry them for another 2 hours. They should be thoroughly dried. Store in a cool place until needed.

To cook noodles, follow directions given on p. 37. Cover with Fresh Tomato Sauce, or any other desired sauce, and sprinkle with cheese. 1½ lbs. of noodles will serve 6.

HOME MADE NOODLES #2

3 cups flour	*3 tablesp. lukewarm water*
6 egg yolks	*½ teasp. salt*

Follow directions for Home Made Noodles #1.

PHILOMENA'S NARROW NOODLES

5 cups flour
4 eggs
¼ cup lukewarm water
½ teasp. salt

Follow directions for Home Made Noodles. This dough may also be used to make Ravioli.

BAKED NOODLES

LASAGNE AL FORNO

1 lb. lasagne
1 cup mozzarella cheese, cut in tiny pieces
2 tablesp. grated Parmesan cheese
1 recipe Chopped Meat Sauce, see p. 55

Prepare Chopped Meat Sauce. Cook lasagne according to directions given under Cooking Hints. Place a layer of drained lasagne in an ungreased casserole. Sprinkle very generously with ½ cup mozzarella and 1 tablesp. grated Parmesan. Pour ½ of the sauce over the cheese, and repeat the layers, using rest of ingredients. Bake in a moderate oven 350° for 15 minutes. Serve immediately. Serves 6.

EGGPLANT WITH LASAGNE: *See p. 147.*

GREEN NOODLES

LASAGNE VERDE

4 cups sifted flour
1 cup pureed spinach
1 recipe Chopped Meat Sauce, see p. 55
½ teasp. salt
2 eggs

Prepare sauce, and while it is cooking, make noodles. Use remaining ingredients, and follow directions for Home Made Noodles, p. 39. Cook noodles in 5 qts. boiling water about 20 to 30 minutes, stirring frequently. Drain, and add 2 tablesp. olive oil. Place one layer of cooked green lasagne in bottom of deep baking dish or casserole. Pour some of the chopped meat sauce over the noodles, and sprinkle with grated Parmesan cheese. Repeat layers until noodles and sauce are used up, ending with sauce and cheese. Bake in moderate oven 350° for ½ hour. Serve immediately. Serves 4.

NOODLES WITH ROMAN SAUCE

TAGLIARINI CON SALSA ALLA ROMANA

4 thin strips salt pork, chopped
2 tablesp. olive oil
12 chicken livers, chopped
2 pairs sweetbreads, parboiled and skinned
½ cup sliced mushrooms
½ cup sherry or marsala
1 6-oz. can tomato paste
2 cups stock
¾ lb. cooked tagliarini (narrow noodles)
¼ lb. butter

Place salt pork, oil, livers, sweetbreads and mushrooms in saucepan, and cook over low flame 5 minutes, stirring frequently. Add wine, and cook 10 to 15 minutes longer, until half of the wine has evaporated. Add tomato paste and stock, and stir until paste is well dissolved. Add seasoning. Cover pan and simmer until thick, about 40 minutes, stirring occasionally. Put cooked tagliarini on a large serving platter, add butter, and mix with two forks until noodles are well covered. Pour sauce over buttered tagliarini, sprinkle with grated cheese, and serve immediately. Enough for 6.

SPAGHETTI WITH ANCHOVIES MILANESE

PASTA ALLA MILANESE CON ACCIUGHI

⅓ cup very finely chopped onion
2 tablesp. olive oil
1 2-oz. can anchovy fillets
1 6-oz. can tomato paste
1 qt. water
2 tablesp. pine nuts
1½ lbs. spaghetti
Salt and pepper

Saute onion in olive oil until light brown. Add anchovies and oil from anchovy can to the onion, and cook to a paste. Add tomato paste and water, and blend well. Season with very little salt, as the anchovies will be salty. Add pine nuts. Cook over a low fire until sauce is thick, about 1 hour, stirring constantly.

Cook spaghetti according to the directions given under Cooking Hints, and put the drained spaghetti on a large platter. Pour sauce over it, and mix until spaghetti is thoroughly moistened. Sprinkle with a topping made of 1 cup toasted bread crumbs mixed with 2 tablesp. grated Romano cheese, and serve at once. Serves 6. This is a popular dish for St. Joseph's Day, March 19th.

SPAGHETTI CASSEROLE

SPAGHETTI IN CASSERUOLA

2 tablesp. olive oil
1 lb. sweet Italian sausage, cut into 1 in. pieces
1 small onion, chopped
¼ lb. mushrooms, sliced
1 #2½ can tomatoes, or tomato puree
Salt and pepper
1 lb. cooked spaghetti
4 slices mozzarella cheese
3 tablesp. grated Parmesan cheese

Brown sausage in oil over medium fire 10 minutes. Add onions, mushrooms, and tomatoes. Season with salt and pepper, and cook uncovered over low fire for 1 hour, stirring occasionally.

While sauce is cooking, prepare spaghetti. Place drained spaghetti in a deep baking pan, and cover with mozzarella slices. Pour sauce over cheese, and sprinkle with grated Parmesan. Bake in a moderate oven 350° until mozzarella is melted, about 10 minutes. Serve immediately. Serves 6.

NOTE: 5 green pitted olives may be added to sauce the last 5 minutes of cooking, if desired.

SPAGHETTI WITH MARINER'S SAUCE

SPAGHETTI MARINARA

3 tablesp. olive oil
1 clove garlic
1 #3 can Italian plum tomatoes
1 tablesp. chopped parsley
1 tablesp. chopped fresh basil
Salt and pepper
1½ lbs. cooked spaghetti
¼ cup grated Parmesan cheese

Saute garlic in oil until light brown, about 3 minutes. Add tomatoes, and mash with a fork until well blended. Sprinkle with parsley and basil, add salt and pepper, and cook uncovered over a low fire for 1 hour, stirring occasionally. Place cooked, drained spaghetti in a deep serving dish, and pour cooked sauce over it. Mix well, sprinkle with grated Parmesan, and serve at once. Serves 6.

NOTE: For a deliciously different taste, add 2 chopped anchovy fillets the last 5 minutes of cooking sauce. A fine herb flavoring may be obtained by adding ½ teasp. oregano 5 minutes before sauce is done.

SPAGHETTINI WITH BUTTER

SPAGHETTINI AL BURRO

1 lb. uncooked spaghettini
5 qts. water
Salt and pepper
¼ lb. butter
½ cup grated Parmesan or Romano cheese

Cook spaghettini in boiling salted water until tender, about 12 minutes. Drain, and place in serving bowl. Melt butter in saucepan and pour it over spaghettini. Season with pepper and cheese, and mix thoroughly, using 2 forks. Serve immediately. Serves 6.

VERMICELLI WITH ZUCCHINI

VERMICELLI CON ZUCCHINI

2 medium-sized zucchini, about 1½ lbs.
¼ cup olive oil
1 small onion, chopped
2 cups fresh peeled tomatoes, cut in small pieces; or,
2 cups canned tomatoes
2 cups water
2 tablesp. chopped fresh basil
½ lb. vermicelli, cut into 1 in. pieces
Salt and pepper

Wash zucchini and scrape lightly with a knife. Cut into 1 in. cubes. Saute onion in oil until light brown, add tomatoes, and simmer for 5 minutes. Add water, and bring to a boil. Add cut-up zucchini and basil. Cook 5 minutes, and add vermicelli. Cook over low fire until pasta is tender, about 15 minutes, stirring occasionally. Season with salt and pepper, and serve hot. Serves 4.

Stuffed Pasta

LITTLE HATS

CAPPELLETTI

Prepare the following stuffing:

1 cup ground round steak
3 tablesp. butter
2 tablesp. grated Parmesan cheese
Salt and pepper

Melt butter in frying pan, add meat, and brown over medium flame for 10 minutes. Remove from stove, add cheese, salt, and pepper, and set aside to cool.

While meat is cooking make the following dough:

2 eggs, slightly beaten
1½ cups sifted flour
¼ teasp. salt
1 tablesp. salad oil

Knead eggs with flour and salt about 1 minute. If dough is too thin, add more flour. Add oil, and form dough into a ball. Divide in two parts, and roll each half out on a lightly floured board to paper thinness. Cut into rounds with a 2 in. cookie cutter, or the top of a glass. Place 1 level teasp. of meat stuffing in center of 1 round, and fold over once to form a little hat. Press edges together with a fork. Cook cappelletti in clear beef or chicken broth for ½ hour in a covered pan. Or, cook in boiling salted water for ½ hour, drain, and serve with Plain Tomato Sauce, see p. 61.

VARIATION: Another filling that may be used is:

½ junket tablet
½ tablesp. cold water
1 cup lukewarm milk
½ lb. ricotta
2 tablesp. minced parsley
Pinch of salt
Pinch of nutmeg

Dissolve junket tablet by crushing it in cold water. Stir into lukewarm milk. Watch temperature of milk closely—if it is too hot the junket will not set. Set aside in a warm place and do not touch for 20 minutes. Then add the ricotta, parsley, salt, and nutmeg, and mix until creamy. Use 1 teasp. filling for each cappelletti.

STUFFED NOODLES

LASAGNE IMBOTTITE

1 lb. pork shoulder butt
1 tablesp. olive oil
1 small onion, chopped
¼ cup burgundy
1 #2½ can Italian plum tomatoes
1 6-oz. can tomato paste
1½ cups cold water
Salt and pepper

Have butcher cut meat into 2 in. cubes. Saute meat in oil over medium flame until brown. Add onion and wine, cover, and cook over low fire until liquid is absorbed, about 1 hour. Add plum tomatoes, and cook over low fire 30 minutes longer. Blend tomato paste with cold water, and add to meat. Add seasonings. Cook 1 hour longer.

While sauce is cooking, prepare the following things:

I.

2 slices dry bread
½ lb. ground beef
¼ lb. ground veal
2 tablesp. grated Parmesan cheese
Salt and pepper
3 tablesp. olive or salad oil

Soak bread in cold water 5 minutes, then squeeze dry with hands. Combine with remaining ingredients, and mix thoroughly. Shape into small balls 1 in. in diameter. Brown meat balls in oil over medium flame for about 6 minutes. Set aside to cool.

II.

2 hard-boiled eggs, chopped

¼ lb. mozzarella cheese, chopped into 1 in. pieces

Combine and set aside.

III.

¼ lb. ricotta

2 tablesp. cold water

Blend ricotta with water until smooth.

IV.

1 lb. lasagne

¼ cup olive oil

Drop lasagne into 5 qts. boiling salted water, and cook for 10 minutes stirring occasionally. Drain, and spread lasagne on a serving platter and pour olive oil over it to prevent the lasagne from sticking to each other.

When sauce is done, pour ½ cup on the bottom of an ungreased baking pan. Sprinkle generously with grated Parmesan. Then put in a layer of lasagne, a layer of meat balls, half the ricotta, and half the egg and mozzarella mixture. Pour on another half cup of tomato sauce, then the remaining other ingredients. Pour the rest of the sauce over all, and sprinkle top with grated Parmesan. Bake in a moderate oven 350° about 20 minutes, cut into portions, and serve immediately. Makes 6 to 8 servings.

VARIATION: 1 pound of Italian sausage may be substituted for meat balls. Cut sausage in 1 in. pieces, and fry in skillet with 1 tablesp. oil for 5 minutes.

RAVIOLI

4 cups sifted flour
½ teasp. salt

5 eggs
¼ cup lukewarm water

Sift flour on to a large board, make a well in center, and add salt, eggs, and water. Knead dough thoroughly about 1

minute, until it is stiff and smooth. Add more flour if dough is too thin. Cover and set aside 10 minutes, while filling is being prepared. Then divide dough into 3 parts, and roll each part out on a lightly floured board to paper thinness. Cut into 2 in. circles with cookie cutter or the top of a glass. Cut 2 rounds for each ravioli. Place a heaping teasp. of desired filling in the center of 1 circle, and cover with another circle. Press edges together with a fork to seal. Cook in 8 qts. boiling salted water until dough is tender. Serve with any tomato or meat sauce, and sprinkle with grated cheese.
NOTE: Ravioli can be cut into 3 and 4 in. squares, if desired. Place filling in center of square, and fold each square over to make a triangle. Press edges with fork to seal.

RAVIOLI FILLINGS:

CHICKEN

RIPIENO RAVIOLI PER POLLO

2 cups cooked chicken breast, chopped
1 egg
½ cup grated Parmesan cheese
2 teasp. minced parsley
1 cup cooked spinach, well drained
Salt and pepper

Combine all ingredients, mixing thoroughly. Use 1 heaping teasp. for each ravioli.

MEAT

1 chopped onion
2 tablesp. olive oil
1 lb. ground pork
1 lb. ground veal
2 tablesp. parsley
¼ cup grated Romano cheese

Saute onion in oil for 2 minutes, add meat, and brown for 5 minutes. Let cool. Add parsley and cheese, and season with salt and pepper, mixing thoroughly. Use 1 heaping teasp. for each ravioli.

RICOTTA #1

1 lb. ground pork
1 teasp. chopped onion
1 cup cooked spinach, well drained
½ cup cracker crumbs
½ lb. ricotta
1 teasp. minced parsley
¼ cup grated Parmesan cheese
2 eggs

Saute meat and onion in skillet over medium flame until brown, stirring constantly. Cool. Combine meat with remaining ingredients, and mix thoroughly. Use 1 heaping teasp. for each ravioli.

RICOTTA #2

1 lb. ricotta
2 eggs, well beaten
2 tablesp. minced parsley
¼ cup grated Parmesan cheese
Salt and pepper

Mix all ingredients together until smooth. Use 1 heaping teasp. for each ravioli.

STUFFED RIGATONI

RIGATONI IMBOTTITE

1 lb. rigatoni
½ lb. chopped veal
½ lb. lean chopped pork
½ cup bread crumbs
¼ cup milk
1 egg
Salt and pepper
One recipe Plain Tomato Sauce, see p. 61
¼ cup grated Parmesan cheese

Cook rigatoni in 5 qts. boiling salted water 10 minutes. Drain well. Combine meat, crumbs, milk, egg, and seasonings, and stuff each rigatoni center with mixture. Push the stuffing in with your finger. Place stuffed rigatoni in baking dish, cover with cooked tomato sauce, and sprinkle with grated Parmesan. Bake in moderate oven 350° 45 minutes. Serve immediately. Serves 6.
NOTE: Tufoli may be used instead of rigatoni.

Dumplings

MRS. BONGIORNO'S DUMPLINGS

GNOCCHI DI SIGNORA BONGIORNO

3 cups hot mashed potatoes (about 5 medium-sized potatoes)
1 cup flour
3 tablesp. grated Parmesan cheese
2 egg yolks

Combine all ingredients in a bowl, and knead until smooth. Roll out on a floured board until ½ in. thick, and cut into 2 in. pieces. Cook in 6 qts. boiling salted water 10 minutes. Drain. Serve with any desired sauce. Enough for 6 people.

PARMESAN DUMPLINGS

GNOCCHI PARMIGIANA

3 cups milk
4 tablesp. butter
½ teasp. salt
½ cup semolina (Cream of Wheat)
2 cups grated Parmesan cheese
1 large egg, or 2 small eggs
½ cup melted butter

Combine milk, butter and salt in a pan. Heat to boiling. Gradually add the semolina to boiling milk, stirring constantly to prevent lumping. Cook over medium fire until thick, about 10 minutes, continuing to stir.

Remove from fire, and add 1 cup grated Parmesan cheese. Add egg, and blend thoroughly. Pour mixture on to a platter, and let it cool until it hardens. When it is firm, take a small piece about the size of an almond. Place your thumb in the center of the piece, and fold it around thumb so that it forms a shell. Or, cut the semolina into 1 inch squares.

Grease the bottom of baking sheet with 3 tablesp. of the melted butter. Arrange shells or squares on sheet in a layer, and pour melted butter over them. Sprinkle with grated cheese. Repeat layers until ingredients are used up. Season each layer with salt and pepper. Bake in moderate oven 375° for 30 to 35 minutes. Serve hot.

NOTE: Dumplings may also be baked with Tomato Mushroom Sauce, Plain Tomato Sauce, or Chopped Meat Sauce. If any of these sauces are used, omit the ½ cup melted butter.

CHICKEN DUMPLINGS

GNOCCHI CON POLLO

5 medium-sized potatoes
1 cup cooked chicken breast, turkey, capon, or veal, ground fine
¼ cup grated Parmesan cheese
¼ teasp. nutmeg
1 cup flour
2 egg yolks
Salt and pepper

Boil potatoes until tender, drain, and mash fine, or put through a ricer. Or, allow to cool and grate. On a bread board combine the potatoes, ground meat or fowl, cheese, nutmeg, flour, egg yolks, and seasonings. Knead until smooth, and if mixture does not hold together, add 1 more egg yolk. If dough is too sticky, add a little more flour. Roll dough out on lightly floured board to ½ in. thickness, and cut into 1 in. pieces. Boil in 8 qts. salted water 10 minutes. Drain and serve with desired sauce. Tomato Sauce or Mushroom Tomato Sauce are especially good.

NOTE: These gnocchi may be poached in boiling chicken or meat broth, and served as accompaniment to soup, if desired.

CHAPTER FIVE

Sauces for Meat, Fish, and Pasta

ANCHOVY SAUCE

ACCIUGHI SALSA

1 2-oz. can anchovy fillet
3 tablesp. olive oil
1 medium-sized onion, chopped
1 #2 can Italian plum tomatoes
Salt and pepper

Drain oil from anchovies and mix in a sauce pan with olive oil. Add onion, and saute over medium fire until brown. Add anchovies and stir to make a paste. Add tomatoes. Cook uncovered over low fire 1 hour, stirring occasionally. Serve hot. Enough for ½ lb. cooked pasta.

ANCHOVY WINE SAUCE

SALSA DI ACCIUGHI E VINO

1 2-oz. can anchovy fillets
1 clove garlic
¼ cup sherry
4 sprigs parsley

Drain oil from anchovies into a pan, and add garlic. Cook anchovies in oil to a paste, remove garlic clove, and add wine. Heat only to boiling, remove from stove, and add parsley. Serve hot or cold on meats and fish. Makes ½ cup.

BARBECUE SAUCE

SALSA PER ARROSTITI

¼ cup minced onion
3 tablesp. wine vinegar
2 tablesp. sugar
½ cup water
1 cup catsup
3 tablesp. Worcestershire sauce

Combine ingredients, and simmer for ten minutes. Makes 1½ cups. May be used on barbecued spareribs or broiled steak.

BOLOGNA SAUCE

SALSA ALLA BOLOGNESE

1 tablesp. butter
½ lb. ground veal
¼ lb. ground ham or salt pork
¼ lb. chicken livers, chopped
1 onion, minced
2 cups stock or water
½ lb. fresh mushrooms, sliced
1 celery stalk, chopped
Salt and pepper
1 tablesp. flour
1 small truffle, sliced (optional)
1 cup light cream

Melt butter over low flame, and add veal, ham or salt pork, chicken livers, and onion, and cook 10 minutes. Add liquid, mushrooms, celery, and seasonings. Cover and simmer for 1 hour, stirring occasionally. Dissolve flour in a little water, and stir into sauce slowly. Add truffle and cook 2 minutes more. Just before serving stir in cream. Use over pasta or rice. Enough for 1 lb. Serves 6.

BROWN SAUCE

SALSA BRUNA

2 tablesp. olive oil
1 tablesp. grated onion
3 mushrooms, chopped
½ cup white wine
Pinch of thyme
½ bay leaf, crushed
1 cup veal or beef stock
Salt and pepper

Saute onion and mushrooms in oil for 3 minutes over low flame. Add wine, thyme, and bay leaf, and cook until wine is reduced to half. Add stock and seasonings, bring to a boil, and boil for 3 minutes. Remove from stove, and strain. Excellent over roasts or steaks. Makes about 1 cup.

CAPER SAUCE

SALSA DI CAPPERI

4 tablesp. butter
2 tablesp. flour
1 cup stock or water
¼ cup capers
2 tablesp. vinegar
Salt and pepper

Melt butter in saucepan, stir in flour, and cook over medium flame 4 minutes, until light brown. Add liquid, capers, vinegar, and seasonings, bring to a boil, and boil 3 minutes, stirring constantly. Serve hot over fish, roast, or fowl. Enough for 2 lbs. meat.

CHOPPED MEAT SAUCE

Follow recipe for sauce in Spaghetti Casserole, p. 42, substituting 1 lb. ground beef for Italian sausage.

CLAM SAUCE

VONGOLI SALSA

1 dozen little neck clams
5 tablesp. olive oil
1 clove garlic, chopped
1 #2½ can Italian plum tomatoes
½ teasp. oregano
Salt and pepper

Scrub clams well with a small vegetable brush, and rinse to remove sand. Open shells by inserting a thin knife between edges. Remove clams and cut them into small pieces, collecting any liquor that drains off. Strain clam liquor into a bowl, and set aside.

Brown garlic in hot oil. Mash tomatoes with fork, add to garlic, and simmer about 2 minutes. Add clam liquor, oregano, and seasonings. Cover and simmer for 45 minutes, stirring occasionally. Add clams and cook about 1 minute more. *Do not overcook clams.* Serve hot over ½ lb. cooked pasta. Serves 4.

GARLIC SAUCE

SALSA DI AGLIO

2 cloves garlic
⅓ cup olive oil
Juice of 2 lemons
1 teasp. oregano
Salt and pepper

Place garlic in wooden bowl and mash. (You may use the bottom of a milk bottle or glass to do this.) Add remaining ingredients. Excellent on broiled chicken, steaks, fish, or lamb. Prepare sauce just before serving time. If desired, mint or basil may be substituted for the oregano.

GARLIC SAUCE FOR PASTA

SALSA DI AGLIO PER PASTA

½ cup olive oil
2 cloves garlic, chopped or whole

Heat oil, and brown garlic until golden brown, about 2 minutes. Add 1 lb. cooked pasta to pan, season with pepper, and simmer about 1 minute. Turn well, so that the pasta is moist with sauce.

HOT PIQUANT SAUCE

SALSA PICCANTE

½ cup olive oil
1 clove garlic (optional)
2 onions, chopped
1 cup Italian red wine, or dry white wine
¼ cup wine vinegar
Pinch of dried red pepper
2 tablesp. capers
Salt and pepper

Combine all ingredients in a jar, and store in refrigerator until wanted. Garlic clove may be removed after 24 hours, if desired. This is an especially good sauce for almost any kind of fish, roast meat, or fowl, or for any kind of game.

LUCANIA SAUCE

SALSA ALLA LUCANIA

3 tablesp. olive oil
1 medium-sized onion, chopped
8 mushrooms, sliced
¼ lb. ground beef
½ cup red wine
2¼ cups water
1 6-oz. can tomato paste
Salt and pepper

Saute onion, mushrooms, and ground beef in oil over low flame, stirring occasionally, until light brown. Add wine, and simmer about 10 minutes, until wine has been reduced to half. Then add water and tomato paste and stir until paste is well dissolved. Season with salt and pepper, and cook uncovered over a low fire until thick, about 1 hour, stirring frequently. Sufficient sauce for 1 lb. rice or pasta. Serves 6.

MINT WINE SAUCE

MENTA VINO SALSA

1 cup white wine *2 tablesp. sugar*
½ cup freshly chopped mint

Mix wine and sugar in saucepan, bring to a boil, and boil 3 minutes over medium flame. Remove from heat, add mint, and let stand one hour. Strain, and serve over fish or meat. Especially good for lamb. Enough sauce for 2 lbs. of meat or fish.

MARINADE FOR GAME

SALSA DI MARINATE

½ cup olive oil
¼ cup Italian red wine
1 teasp. salt
Pinch of oregano
½ teasp. pepper
1 clove garlic

Combine all ingredients, and store in icebox in a jar. Shake well before using. Marinate meat in this sauce for at least 2 hours.

PINE NUT SAUCE #1

SALSA PIGNOLI

1 tablesp. pine nuts, shelled
2 tablesp. raisins or currants
½ cup wine vinegar
1 cup water
1 tablesp. mint, parsley, or basil, chopped
Salt and pepper

Combine all ingredients in a sauce pan and cook for 7 minutes over medium heat. Pour over fried, baked, or broiled fish. Makes 1 cup. Serves 6.

PINE NUT SAUCE #2

SALSA PIGNOLI

2 anchovy fillets
1 tablesp. pine nuts, shelled
1 hard-boiled egg yolk
¼ clove garlic
2 chopped olives, pitted
2 sprigs parsley, chopped
1 tablesp. bread crumbs
1 tablesp. vinegar
½ cup olive oil
1 raw egg yolk
2 tablesp. wine vinegar
Pepper

Put anchovies, pine nuts, hard-boiled egg yolk, garlic, olives, and parsley through a food chopper, using finest blade. Moisten crumbs with vinegar, and add to chopped ingredients. Add olive oil, pepper, and raw egg yolk, and beat with rotary beater for 3 minutes. Rub through a fine sieve. Just before serving, add 2 tablesp. wine vinegar and stir well. A thick sauce which is excellent for any kind of meat, roast, fowl, or fish. Makes 1½ cups.

SARDINE SAUCE WITH FENNEL

SARDINE SALSA CON FENNEL

1 lb. fresh sardines
¼ cup olive oil
1 clove garlic
1 qt. water
1 teasp. shelled pine nuts
Salt and pepper
1 lb. fresh fennel, chopped
1 lb. cooked pasta
1 cup toasted bread crumbs

Have fish dealer clean sardines, removing head and bones. Brown garlic in hot oil 3 minutes. Add sardines, and saute, turning constantly, until light brown. Add water, pine nuts, salt, and pepper, and cook over low heat 5 minutes. Add fennel to fish, and cook covered 15 minutes over low flame, stirring occasionally to prevent sticking.

Pour half the cooked sauce over cooked, drained pasta, and sprinkle half the crumbs over pasta. Reserve the other half of sauce and crumbs to pass at the table for individual servings. Serve hot. Serves 6. Sicilians traditionally serve pasta with this sauce on St. Joseph's Day, March 19th.

BASIC SWEET AND SOUR SAUCE

SALSA FONDAMENTALE DI ARGO E DOLCE

½ lb. onions, sliced thin
¼ cup olive oil
¼ cup wine vinegar
1 teasp. sugar
Salt and pepper

Saute sliced onions in oil 5 minutes over low flame. Blend vinegar and sugar and pour over onions. Season with salt and pepper, cover pan, and cook over low flame until onions are tender, about 3 minutes. Serve this sauce with fish, or liver, or use it to marinate fish and liver before cooking. Enough for 2 lbs.

TOMATO SAUCE

SALSA SEMPLICE DI POMODORO

Probably the best known of all Italian sauces is the basic tomato sauce. It is usually served with meat or pasta—spaghetti and meat balls with a tomato sauce have probably been eaten by almost everyone. Tomato sauce may also be used with fish. There are many variations, as you will see from reading this chapter; but there are some tricks to help you make a good tomato sauce, which are:

1. Use an enamel or stainless steel pan to cook in.
2. Simmer sauce. Do not cook over high heat.
3. Cook sauce uncovered, stirring occasionally.
4. If a fatty meat is one of the ingredients of the sauce, or if it is cooked in the sauce, skim off some of the melted fat which will rise to the surface during cooking.

BASIC TOMATO SAUCE FOR MEAT

¼ cup olive oil or salad oil
1 medium-sized onion, chopped
2 6-oz. cans tomato paste
6 cups water
Salt and pepper

Heat oil in large enamel or stainless steel saucepan. Brown onions in oil until soft. Add tomato paste and water, and stir until well blended. Add seasonings, and simmer uncovered until sauce is thick, about 2½ hours. This sauce may be served over meat; or, you can use it without meat for pasta. Enough for 1 lb. of pasta.

PLAIN TOMATO SAUCE

3 tablesp. olive oil
1 small onion, chopped
1 6-oz. can tomato paste
1 #2½ can Italian plum tomatoes, strained
3 cups water
Salt and pepper
½ bay leaf (optional)
½ teasp. oregano (optional)

Saute onion in oil in enamel or stainless steel saucepan until soft. Add tomato paste, strained tomatoes, and water. Stir until well blended, add seasonings, and cook uncovered over low flame until thick, about 1 hour. Enough for 1 lb. any kind of pasta. Serves 6.

FRESH TOMATO SAUCE

SALSA SEMPLICE DI SOLO FRESCO POMODORO

4 lbs. ripe fresh tomatoes
¼ cup olive oil
2 cloves garlic, chopped; or 1 small onion, chopped
2 sprigs fresh sweet basil, chopped
Salt and pepper

Cut tomatoes into small wedges, and cook in enamel or stainless steel pan for 10 minutes over medium fire, until tomatoes are soft. Cool, and rub through strainer. Brown garlic in hot oil until golden brown. Add tomato puree and seasonings. Cook uncovered until thick about 1½ hours, stirring occasionally. Makes enough to cover 1 lb. of any kind of pasta. Serves 6.

TRUFFLE SAUCE

SALSA TARTUFATA

2 tablesp. butter
1 onion, chopped
½ clove garlic
2 sprigs parsley, chopped
1 cup stock or water
1 tablesp. flour
¼ cup white wine
Salt and pepper
6 peeled truffles, sliced thin

Saute onion, garlic, and parsley in butter until light brown. Dissolve flour in wine, and add with stock to pan. Add seasonings, and simmer uncovered 15 minutes. Add truffles, and cook 5 minutes more. Serve hot. Especially good with roast veal or fowl. Makes 1¼ cups.

WINE SAUCE FOR MEAT

SALSA VINO

1 tablesp. onion, chopped; or,
1 clove garlic, chopped
2 tablesp. olive oil
2 tablesp. wine vinegar
1 cup white wine
Pinch of rosemary
Salt and pepper

Place all ingredients in a bottle, and store in icebox until needed. Use it to baste fowl and veal during cooking. Substitute red wine if you desire a wine sauce for beef, pork, or lamb.

CHAPTER SIX

Meats

Beef

BEEF WITH MUSHROOMS

BUE CON FUNGHI

2 lbs. eye round of beef, in 1 piece
6 tablesp. lard or olive oil
Salt and pepper
2 tablesp. butter
½ lb. mushrooms, sliced
1 small onion, sliced
1 cup sherry or marsala

Have butcher lard beef with pork fat and tie with string. Sear meat in hot lard or oil, then place in a shallow baking pan, sprinkle with salt and pepper, and cook in a slow oven 325° 30 to 35 minutes, until tender. Turn once during roasting.

While meat is cooking prepare mushroom sauce. Saute mushrooms in butter until brown. Add sliced onions, cover, and cook 3 minutes longer, until onions are tender. Just before serving, add wine to mushrooms and heat, but do not boil. Transfer meat to hot platter, slice into serving pieces, and pour mushroom sauce over slices. Serve immediately. Serves 4.

FILET MIGNON ITALIAN STYLE

FILETTO DI BUE

2 lbs. filet mignon
2 slices bacon or suet
1 small onion, sliced
Salt and pepper
¼ cup melted butter
½ cup madeira or sherry

Fry bacon slices 1 minute, add onions, and saute until light brown. Remove bacon and onion from pan, and brown meat in drippings over high flame on both sides. Reduce heat to medium and cook 5 minutes longer. Do not overcook; filet should be rare or medium. Pour melted butter over filet in pan, add wine, and cook 1 minute longer. Serve immediately. Serves 6.

BARBECUED HAMBURGER (SPECIAL)

3 tablesp. olive oil
2 lbs. ground beef
1 medium-sized onion, chopped fine
3 tablesp. Worcestershire sauce
3 tablesp. wine vinegar
2 tablesp. sugar
½ cup water
1 12-oz. bottle catsup
Salt and pepper
1 loaf of Italian bread

Saute ground beef in hot oil over medium flame until well browned, about 8 minutes, stirring with a fork until pieces are broken up. Combine remaining ingredients and pour over browned meat, reduce heat, and simmer 20 minutes, stirring frequently. Cut loaf of Italian bread into pieces 4 in. long (or split 8 hamburger rolls in half), and spread 2 heaping tablespoons of barbecued meat on each piece of bread. Serve immediately. Serves 8. The meat will be moist and delicious.

MEAT BALLS #1

POLPETTE

2 lbs. ground beef
2 eggs
½ cup breadcrumbs
1 tablesp. chopped onion
¼ cup grated Romano or Parmesan cheese
2 sprigs parsley, chopped
Salt and pepper
1 recipe Basic Tomato Sauce, p. 61

Combine ingredients, except sauce, and mix thoroughly. With hands shape into balls about the size of an egg. Place in frying pan with ¼ cup of salad or olive oil, and brown over medium flame. Remove and place in sauce which has been heated to boiling. Simmer meat balls in sauce uncovered, until well done, about 2½ hours. Serve with pasta and pour sauce over both.

VARIATIONS: 1. To make softer meat balls, substitute 4 slices of dry bread soaked in water and squeezed dry for the ½ cup bread crumbs.

2. 1¼ lbs. ground beef and ½ lb. ground pork may be used instead of all beef.
3. ½ lb. ground pork, ½ lb. ground veal, and 1 lb. ground beef may be used instead of all beef.
4. 1 lb. ground pork, and 1 lb. of ground veal may be used instead of all beef.

STUFFED MEAT LOAF

POLPETTONE IMBOTTITE

1 lb. ground lean beef; or ½ lb. ground beef and ½ lb. ground pork
1 tablesp. chopped parsley
Salt and pepper
4 thin slices prosciutto
1 cup mashed potatoes; or 1 cup ricotta
¼ lb. mozzarella cheese, sliced thin
4 tablesp. olive oil
1 6-oz. can tomato paste
3 cups water

Combine ground meat, parsley, salt and pepper, and mix well. Dust a bread board with flour, and flatten meat on it until it is about 5 by 8 in. Place prosciutto slices on flattened meat, then spread mashed potatoes or ricotta, and then the slices of mozzarella. Roll meat like a jelly roll, and pinch edges closed. Pour 2 tablesp. olive oil into a large frying pan. Heat oil, then place meat loaf in pan, and pour balance of oil over loaf. Cover pan tightly, and simmer 15 minutes until meat is lightly browned. Add tomato paste which has been mixed well with water, bay leaf, salt, and pepper. Cover pan and simmer 1 hour. Remove loaf from pan gently with pancake turner, and allow to cool 15 minutes before slicing it into serving pieces. If you try to cut it while it is too hot, it will fall apart. Serve with tomato sauce from pan. Serves 4.

POT ROAST

FETTA DI MANZO

1½ lbs. chuck roast
½ cup olive or salad oil
1 clove garlic
1 #2 can Italian plum tomatoes
½ bay leaf; or, 1 teasp. fresh or dried rosemary
Salt and pepper

Brown garlic in oil for 2 minutes over medium flame. Remove garlic from pan, and brown meat on all sides for 10 minutes. Add tomatoes, bay leaf, and seasoning. Cover pan tightly and simmer until meat is tender, about 2½ hours. Add a little water or stock if pan get dry. Serves 4.

VARIATIONS: 6 small peeled potatoes may be added 25 minutes before meat is done. Or, ½ lb. fresh mushrooms, sliced, may be added with tomatoes.

POT ROAST, PIEDMONT STYLE

MANZO USO PIEMONTESE

1 rib roast, about 3½ lbs.
6 slices of prosciutto for larding
2 slices prosciutto, chopped
1 truffle, sliced (optional)
2 tablesp. butter
1 carrot, diced
1 clove garlic
1 celery stalk, chopped
2 tablesp. minced parsley
1 onion, chopped
1 tablesp. tomato paste
2 cups stock or water
½ cup sherry
Salt and pepper

Have butcher remove bone from roast, and lard meat with 6 slices prosciutto. Place sliced truffles on meat, roll up, and tie with string. Brown meat in butter, add chopped prosciutto, carrot, garlic, celery, parsley, and onion. Dilute tomato paste in stock or water, add to meat, and add wine and seasonings. Cook covered over low flame until tender, 2 to 3 hours. Pour meat and liquid over ½ lb. cooked rice, or pasta. Serve hot. Serves 4.

BEEF ROLLS

BRACIUOLINI

There are many variations of braciuolini, and practically every Italian homemaker has her own favorite. Below are two of the most popular recipes. The most efficient way to make beef rolls is to start the sauce first. While it is simmering, prepare the meat. Then, after the braciuolini are all ready to cook, add them to the partially done sauce, and finish both together.

TOMATO SAUCE FOR BRACIUOLINI

2 tablesp. olive oil
1 clove garlic
1 #2½ can Italian plum tomatoes
1 6-oz. can tomato paste
3 cups water
Salt and pepper

Heat oil, and brown garlic until golden brown. Add plum tomatoes, tomato paste, and water. Blend well, season with salt and pepper, and cover pan. Simmer sauce until braciuolini are prepared. Then bring sauce to a boil, add beef rolls and drippings from their preparation to sauce, and cook slowly until meat is tender, about 2 hours.

BRACIUOLINI #1

1½ lbs. top round steak, cut in slices
2 tablesp. grated Parmesan cheese
1 clove garlic
⅓ tablesp. salt
Pinch of pepper
1 teasp. chopped parsley
2 tablesp. olive oil
2 pieces of pork fat, about ½ inch wide by 3 inches long, or 2 slices of bacon

Slices of meat should be about 8 by 9 inches. Place meat on board. Combine cheese, garlic, salt, pepper, parsley, and oil. Mix together until paste is formed. Spread meat with mixture, top with pork fat or bacon, and roll each slice of meat like a jelly roll. Roll from the short side as tightly as possible, and tie securely with a soft white string. Brown meat in hot olive oil. Add meat and drippings to tomato sauce. Cook slowly until meat is tender, about 2 hours. Remove meat from sauce and cool for 5 minutes. Slice meat crosswise into ¾ in. slices. Pour ½ cup of cooked sauce over meat slices, and pour remaining sauce over 1 lb. of cooked pasta. Sprinkle with grated cheese, and serve immediately. Serves 6.

BRACIUOLINI #2

1½ lbs. top round steak, cut in slices
¼ cup bread crumbs
3 tablesp. grated Romano cheese
1 teasp. fresh or dried sweet basil
1 slice salami ⅛th in. thick, diced
1 clove garlic, slivered; or, 1 teasp. chopped onion
Salt and pepper
2 slices bacon
2 hard-boiled eggs, sliced

Combine crumbs, cheese, basil, salami, and garlic or onion. Lay slices of meat flat, sprinkle with salt and pepper, and spread with crumb mixture. Place bacon slices on top of crumbs, and put slices of hard-boiled egg on bacon. Roll up. Cook as directed for Braciuolini #1.

STEAK SICILIAN STYLE

BISTECCA ALLA SICILIANA

2 T-bone, sirloin, or minute steaks
2 cloves garlic
1 cup olive oil
3 tablesp. grated Parmesan cheese
1 cup bread crumbs
Salt and pepper

Crush garlic in bowl, add oil, and blend well. Dip steaks in garlic and oil. Combine cheese, crumbs and seasonings, and roll steaks in crumbs. Grill or broil steaks until they have reached desired degree of rareness. Serves 2.

BROILED STEAK ROLLS

FILETTO BRACIUOLINI ALLA GRIGLIA

2 lbs. tender beef steak
2 sprigs parsley, chopped
1 cup soft bread crumbs
¼ lb. prosciutto, minced
1 onion, grated
Salt and pepper
1 tablesp. grated Parmesan or Romano cheese
¼ lb. mozzarella cheese, cut in 1 in. squares
6 slices white bread, diced
½ cup flour
2 eggs slightly beaten
1 cup grated bread crumbs
4 tablesp. olive oil

Cut steak into 8 slices 3 in. wide, and flatten them to ¼ to ½ in. thick. Have ten skewers ready. Combine parsley, bread crumbs, prosciutto, onion, grated cheese and seasonings. Place some of this mixture on each of the meat slices, and roll slices up like jelly roll. Place 1 meat roll, 1 square of mozzarella, and 1 square of bread on a skewer, roll each skewer lightly in flour, dip it in beaten eggs, and then roll in bread crumbs. Brush with olive oil, and place skewer on a preheated broiling rack. Broil slowly about 5 minutes, then turn skewer, and broil other side 5 minutes. Serve hot on skewers. Serves 6.

SKEWERED MEAT ROMAN STYLE

SPIEDINI ALLA ROMANA

I.

1 lb. ground beef
½ cup bread crumbs
2 eggs
2 tablesp. grated Parmesan cheese
2 tablesp. chopped parsley
1 clove garlic, chopped
1 teasp. finely chopped onion
Salt and pepper

Combine all ingredients and shape into oblong rolls 1 in. thick. Set aside until ready to use.

II.

½ loaf Italian bread, sliced ¼ in. thick; or, any white bread, cut into 1 in. cubes
1 lb. mozzarella cheese, cut into 1 in. cubes
¼ lb. prosciutto or salami, cut into 1 in. cubes
½ cup flour
2 eggs, well beaten
1 cup bread crumbs

Use 12 small skewers. On each skewer put a roll of chopped meat mixture, 1 cube of bread, 1 cube of mozzarella, and 1 cube of prosciutto or salami. Dip filled skewers in flour, then in beaten eggs, and finally in crumbs.

Heat ¾ cup salad oil in deep frying pan, and fry filled skewers until brown, 4 or 5 minutes on each side. Turn gently, and watch carefully. Serve immediately on skewers, accompanied by boiled rice and a green salad. Serves 6.

VARIATION: If desired, 1 lb. of either pork, beef, lamb, or veal may be cubed, and substituted for the ground meat mixture. Omit all other ingredients of Part I, and thread skewers with cubes of meat, cheese, bread, and ham or salami. Follow cooking directions in Part II.

VEAL WITH ANCHOVIES AND TUNA

VITELLO CON ACCIUGHE E TONNATO

2½ lbs. lean veal, in 1 piece
4 large salted anchovies
1 teasp. salt
1 small onion
2 medium-sized carrots
1 celery stalk with leaves, halved
1 bay leaf
Pinch of pepper
1 3½-oz. can tuna fish in olive oil
¼ cup olive oil
Juice of 1 lemon
1 tablesp. capers (optional)

Wash anchovies in cold water, remove head, tail, and backbone, and cut into 8 strips. Place 4 anchovy strips on inner side of meat, roll up like jelly roll, and tie with string. Fill a large kettle with water, add salt, onion, carrots, celery, bay leaf, and pepper. Bring to a boil and add veal. Simmer covered until meat is tender, about 1½ hours. Skim surface during cooking. Remove cooked meat from broth, and drain. Strain broth. Slice meat thin, and place slices close together in an earthenware casserole large enough to hold meat and sauce. Cover casserole and set in refrigerator for 2 days. Serve veal with the following sauce:

Pound together in a mortar the remaining 4 strips of anchovies, and the tuna fish. Add oil, lemon juice, and capers. Blend well. Pour over veal. Serves 6.

NOTE: This dish has a tangy and unusual taste. It will keep almost a week if refrigerated, and it is especially delightful on a hot summer day.

BAKED VEAL CUTLETS

VITELLO IMBOTTITO AL FORNO

1 lb. veal cutlets
¾ cup olive oil
1 cup bread crumbs
Salt and pepper
3 tablesp. grated Parmesan cheese (optional)
2 large onions, sliced
1 #2 can tomatoes

Cut meat into 3 in. squares, and dip in oil. Combine crumbs, salt, pepper, and cheese, and roll cutlets in this mixture. Grease a baking dish or casserole with oil. Put ½ sliced onion on the bottom of the pan, then a layer of veal, and top with a layer of tomatoes which have been mashed well with a fork. Repeat until all ingredients are used. Bake in moderate oven 375° until onions and meat are tender, about 30 minutes. Serve hot. Serves 4.

VARIATION: Potatoes may be added if desired. Use 2 medium-sized potatoes, peeled and cut crosswise into ¼ in.

slices. Insert a layer of potatoes between onions and meat, and proceed as above.

VEAL CUTLETS MILANESE

COTOLETTE ALLA MILANESE

1 lb. veal cutlets
½ cup flour
2 egg yolks
Salt and pepper
1 cup bread crumbs
¼ cup butter
4 lemon wedges

Pound cutlets thin, and roll in flour. Beat egg yolks slightly, and add salt and pepper. Dip floured cutlets in beaten eggs, and then roll in bread crumbs. Fry cutlets in butter over medium flame until golden brown on both sides. Serve immediately, garnished with lemon wedges. Serves 4.

VEAL DUMPLINGS: *See p. 36.*

VEAL FLORENTINE STYLE

VITELLO ALLA FIORENTINA

2 lbs. rump veal, cubed
1 small onion, sliced
¼ cup olive oil
1 clove garlic
1 cup canned tomatoes
Pinch of rosemary
¼ cup white wine
Salt and pepper

Fry onion in oil for 2 minutes; add garlic, and brown 1 minute longer. Add meat and brown well on all sides over medium flame. Add remaining ingredients, cover pan, and cook over low flame until meat is tender, about 30 minutes. Stir occasionally. Serve hot over rice or mashed potatoes. Serves 4.

VEAL MOZZARELLA

VITELLO ALLA MOZZARELLA

4 slices veal, 4 in. by ¼ in.
2 eggs
1 cup bread crumbs
1 tablesp. chopped parsley
2 tablesp. grated Romano cheese
Salt and pepper
⅓ cup olive or salad oil
1 cup Plain Tomato Sauce, see p. 61
4 slices mozzarella cheese, ¼ in. thick

Beat eggs slightly. Combine crumbs, parsley, cheese, salt and pepper. Dip veal in eggs, then roll in crumbs. Brown cutlets in oil on both sides over medium flame. Transfer to a baking dish, and pour tomato sauce over them. Place 1 slice mozzarella on each cutlet, and bake in a slow oven 250° until cheese is bubbling hot, about 15 to 20 minutes. Cheese should be lightly browned. Serve immediately. Serves 4.

VEAL PARMESAN

VITELLO ALLA PARMIGIANA

1 lb. veal cutlets
¼ cup oil or butter
1 clove garlic; or, 1 small onion, chopped
½ cup sliced mushrooms
Salt and pepper
½ cup marsala, sherry, or madeira
½ cup grated Parmesan cheese

Have butcher flatten meat to ¼ in. thick, and cut it into 3 in. pieces. Brown in oil or butter over high heat on both sides, and transfer to a baking dish. Keep warm while you prepare sauce. Saute garlic and mushrooms in same oil as veal over low flame until soft. Season with salt and pepper, remove pan from fire, and stir in wine and cheese. Pour sauce over veal and bake in moderate oven 325° until meat is tender and bubbling hot. Serve very hot with pasta. Serves 4.

VARIATION: Slice 1 ripe, firm tomato over browned meat before adding mushroom sauce. Or, cover each cutlet with a slice of prosciutto before adding sauce.

VEAL ROMAN STYLE

SALTIMBOCCA ALLA ROMANA

2 lbs. veal cutlets
10 to 12 thin slices prosciutto
10 to 12 slices mozzarella
½ teasp. sage
Salt and pepper
¼ lb. butter
½ cup marsala

Flatten veal very thin and cut it into 3 in. pieces. Put 1 slice prosciutto, 1 slice mozzarella, and a pinch of sage on a piece of veal, and cover with a second piece of veal, sandwich style. Sprinkle lightly with salt and pepper and skewer with toothpicks. Saute in butter over medium flame, until golden brown on both sides, about 10 minutes. Remove from pan and keep hot. Add wine to drippings in pan and heat, but do not boil. Pour sauce over cutlets and serve immediately. Serves 4.

VEAL SCALOPPINE

1 lb. veal cutlets
¼ cup flour
Salt and pepper
3 tablesp. olive or salad oil
2 teasp. lemon juice
1 cup white wine or marsala

Flatten meat with edge of heavy plate or meat hammer until it is not more than ⅛th in. thick. Cut into serving pieces. Combine flour, salt, and pepper, and dredge meat lightly. Brown well in hot oil over high flame, about 2 minutes on each side. Blend lemon juice and wine, and pour over browned cutlets. Reduce heat to low, cover pan, and cook for 2 or 3 minutes. Do not allow to boil. Serve immediately. Serves 4.

VEAL SCALOPPINE CALABRESE STYLE

SCALOPPINE ALLA CALABRESE

1 lb. veal rump
6 tablesp. olive oil
1 cup sliced mushrooms
1 #2 can tomatoes
Salt and pepper
2 large green peppers, cut in 1 in. strips
1 red pepper, coarsely chopped

Cut meat into 1½ in. cubes, and saute in 3 tablesp. olive oil over medium flame until brown on all sides. Add mushrooms and strained tomatoes, cover pan, and simmer 10 minutes. Fry peppers in remaining 3 tablesp. of oil for about 15 minutes, stirring occasionally. Add peppers to meat and cook 15 minutes longer over medium flame. Serve hot. Serves 4.

NOTE: If a thicker sauce is desired, use 1 #2 can tomato puree instead of tomatoes.

STUFFED VEAL BREAST

VITELLO IMBOTTITO

1 veal breast, about 3 lbs.
2 slices bread
½ lb. ground pork
¼ lb. ground beef
1 egg
1 tablesp. chopped parsley
¼ lb. mozzarella cheese, diced
Salt and pepper
4 slices salt pork or bacon
1 #2 can tomatoes
1 tablesp. oregano

Have butcher make a pocket in veal breast. Soak bread in cold water 5 minutes, squeeze dry, and combine with pork, beef, egg, parsley, cheese, salt, and pepper. Mix well with hands. Wipe meat with damp cloth, stuff cavity, and sew or skewer closed. Place meat in roasting pan, and cover with slices of pork or bacon. Roast in covered pan in moderate

oven 350° until tender, about 2 hours. Remove from oven and let cool at room temperature 10 minutes. Slice into serving pieces, and place these back into roasting pan. Spread top of slices with drained tomatoes, sprinkle with oregano, and roast uncovered for 20 minutes. Serve hot. Serves 4.
VARIATION: Use ¾ lb. Italian sausage instead of ground pork and beef. Use very little salt.

Variety Meats

BRAINS WITH EGGS

CERVELLI CON UOVA

½ lb. calves brains
1 tablesp. salad oil
4 eggs
1 tablesp. grated Parmesan cheese
Salt and pepper

Soak brains in cold water 1 hour. Drain, and remove membranes. Chop into 1 in. cubes. Fry in oil over low flame about 10 minutes, turning with a spoon until evenly browned. Break eggs into a bowl, add remaining ingredients, and beat lightly with a fork. Pour eggs over brains, and cook, stirring constantly, until eggs are set. Serve hot. Serves 2.

BRAINS WITH WINE

CERVELLI CON VINO

½ lb. lamb, pork, or beef brains
¼ cup Italian red wine

Soak brains in cold water 1 hour, drain, and remove membrane. Saute in oil until browned, and then add wine. Cook slowly until wine is hot. Do not boil. Serve immediately. Serves 2.

KIDNEYS WITH ONIONS

ARNIONE CON CIPOLLA

3 kidneys, about 1 lb.
4 tablesp. salad oil
4 medium-sized onions, sliced
Salt and pepper

Split kidneys lengthwise through center. Remove membranes, fat, and white tubes. Slice into ¼ in. slices, and cover with cold water to which 1 teasp. salt has been added. Soak 1 hour, then rinse well. Saute onion in oil, add kidneys and seasonings. Cover pan and simmer until tender, about 25 to 30 minutes. If pan becomes too dry, add 2 tablesp. water. Serve immediately. Serves 4.

Do not overcook kidneys, or they will be tough.

KIDNEYS WITH MUSHROOMS

ARNIONE CON FUNGHI

2 kidneys
½ lb. fresh button mushrooms
2 tablesp. salad oil
Salt and pepper

Split kidneys lengthwise through center. Remove membranes, fat, and white tubes. Slice into ½ in. slices, and soak in cold water 10 minutes. Rinse, and drain. Wipe mushrooms with damp cloth, and saute with kidneys in oil over low flame for 5 to 7 minutes. Stir occasionally. Serve hot. Serves 2.

BROILED LIVER

FEGATO ALLA GRIGLIA

1 lb. calves liver
2 tablesp. salad oil
Salt and pepper

Have butcher slice liver ½ to ¾ in. thick. Brush lightly with oil, sprinkle with salt and pepper, and broil on a rack 3 in. from flame. Broil 5 to 6 minutes, but do not overcook or liver will become tough. Liver slices should be golden brown on both sides. Serve hot. Serves 4.

VARIATION: Serve liver with the following wine sauce:

2 tablesp. salad oil
1 large onion, sliced thin
½ cup Italian red wine

Saute onions in oil until soft. Add wine, and heat for 1 minute, but do not boil. Spread over liver and serve at once.

FRIED LIVER

FEGATO FRITTO

1 lb. liver, sliced thin
1 egg, well beaten
¼ cup bread crumbs
Salt and pepper
3 tablesp. olive or salad oil

Dip liver in beaten egg, then in crumbs and seasonings. Fry liver in oil 1 minute over high flame, turn, and cook other side. Reduce heat to low, and cook 3 minutes more until brown. Serve immediately garnished with lemon wedges. Serves 4.

LIVER MILANESE

FEGATO ALLA MILANESE

1 lb. calf, beef, or pork liver, sliced ¾ in. thick
Salt and pepper
4 tablesp. flour
5 tablesp. olive oil
1 large onion, sliced
½ lb. mushrooms, sliced
2 tablesp. tomato paste (optional)
¼ cup water, stock, or claret

Sprinkle liver with salt and pepper, and roll in flour. Brown liver in oil over high flame for 2 minutes on each side. Remove from pan and keep warm until ready to serve. *Do not overcook.* Saute onion and mushrooms in same oil, stirring occasionally. Dilute tomato paste with water or stock, add, and continue cooking 5 minutes. Add liver, and cook 2 minutes longer. Serve hot. Serves 4.

LIVER SWEET AND SOUR

FEGATO DOLCE E AGRO

1 lb. liver, sliced ½ in. thick
Salt and pepper
2 tablesp. olive oil

Sprinkle liver with salt and pepper, and saute in oil 2 minutes over a high flame. Reduce heat, and cook 3 minutes more. Prepare Sweet Sour Sauce in separate pan:

4 tablesp. olive oil
2 medium-sized onions, sliced
1 teasp. sugar
2 tablesp. wine vinegar
Pinch of salt and pepper

Saute onion in oil over low flame until soft. Add vinegar and remaining ingredients. Heat thoroughly, stir, and add to pan with liver. Cook slowly until liver is tender, about 1 minute more. Serve immediately. Serves 4.

LIVER VENETIAN STYLE

FEGATO ALLA VENEZIA

1 lb. calves liver
2 medium-sized onions, sliced thin
Salt and pepper
1 teasp. fresh mint or parsley, chopped

Have butcher slice liver ¾ in. thick. Cut into 2 in. squares. Saute onions in butter until soft, add liver, and sprinkle with salt and pepper. Fry over high flame until brown on all sides, about 3 minutes. Remove from heat, sprinkle with mint or parsley, and serve immediately. Serves 4.

TONGUE

LINGUA

2 veal tongues, about 4 lbs.
2 teasp. salt
2 onions, chopped
1 bay leaf
1 carrot, chopped
1 celery stalk, chopped

Place tongues in large pot, cover with cold water, and add remaining ingredients. Cook covered over low fire until tongue skin curls back, about 1½ hours. Drain, and reserve liquid to use as stock. Cool tongue, and when cool enough to handle, remove skin and any excess fat. Slice and serve either hot or cold. Good with the following sauce:

WINE SAUCE FOR TONGUE

SALSA VINO

1 teasp. sugar
1 tablesp. wine vinegar
1 cup sauterne
2 tablesp. grated unsweetened chocolate
2 tablesp. raisins
2 tablesp. shelled pine nuts

Combine sugar and vinegar and cook over low fire until sugar is dissolved. Do not allow to boil. Add remaining ingredients, bring to a boil, and cook, stirring constantly, until chocolate is melted. Pour sauce over sliced tongue, and serve hot. Serves 8.

TRIPE BOLOGNA

TRIPPA ALLA BOLOGNESE

1 lb. tripe, cut into thin strips
1 teasp. salt
3 tablesp. olive oil or butter
3 eggs, slightly beaten
3 tablesp. grated Parmesan cheese
1 tablesp. parsley, chopped
1 teasp. lemon juice
Salt and pepper

Wash tripe several times in cold water. Cook slowly in lightly salted water to cover for 1 hour. Drain. Heat oil in frying pan and brown tripe over low flame, stirring occasionally. Combine remaining ingredients, pour over tripe, and continue to cook, stirring constantly, until eggs are set. Serve immediately. Serves 4.

MIXED FRY

FRITTO MISTO

½ lb. calf's sweetbreads
½ lb. calf's liver
3 tablesp. oil or butter
Salt and pepper
Lemon wedges

Parboil sweetbreads 5 minutes, remove from flame, and plunge them into cold water. Dry, and cut off membranes. Cut sweetbreads and liver into 1 in. pieces. Fry sweetbreads and liver in hot oil over medium fire until brown on both sides, about 5 minutes. Season with salt and pepper, and garnish with lemon wedges. Serve immediately. Serves 4.

SWEETBREADS WITH MARSALA

ANIMELLA CON MARSALA

1 lb. sweetbreads
3 tablesp. butter
Salt and pepper
3 tablesp. marsala

Soak sweetbreads in cold water to cover for 30 minutes. Drain, place in a saucepan with cold water, cover pan, and cook slowly for 20 minutes. *Do not boil.* Drain, and plunge into a bowl of cold water. When cool, remove membrane and slice lengthwise into 3 in. slices. Melt butter in frying pan, add sweetbreads, and saute until delicately browned, about 8 minutes. Season with salt and pepper, and add wine. Cook 2 minutes longer. Serve hot. Serves 4.

FRIED SWEETBREADS

ANIMELLA FRITTI

1 lb. sweetbreads
½ cup bread crumbs
2 tablesp. grated Parmesan cheese
Salt and pepper
1 egg, well beaten
½ cup salad oil

Parboil sweetbreads as directed in Sweetbreads with Marsala, and cut into 3 in. slices. Combine crumbs, cheese, and seasonings, and roll sweetbreads in crumbs, then dip in egg, and then roll in crumbs again. Saute sweetbreads in oil over medium flame 10 minutes, until golden brown. Serve hot. Serves 6.

Lamb

LAMB NEAPOLITAN STYLE

AGNELLO ALLA NAPOLETINA

1 small leg of lamb, 3 to 4 lbs.
1 slice salt pork, ½ in. thick.
¼ cup olive oil or butter
1 clove garlic
1 medium-sized onion, chopped
¼ cup fresh mint, chopped; or, 1 teasp. dried rosemary
1 cup stock or water
1 tablesp. brandy or sherry
1 cup tomato puree or tomato juice

Have leg of lamb boned. Place pork slice in center of lamb, and roll up like a jelly roll. Tie with string. Sprinkle meat with salt and pepper, and brown on all sides in a heavy pan or Dutch oven over medium heat, turning often. Add garlic and onion, and saute until golden brown. Add mint or rosemary, liquid, brandy, and tomato puree. Cover pan tightly and simmer until meat is tender, 1½ to 2 hours. Turn occasionally. Add a little more stock if necessary from time to time. Serve lamb with pan gravy, skimming off the excess fat. Serve hot. Serves 6.

LAMB PEASANT STYLE

AGNELLO ALLA PAESANA

2 lbs. lean stew lamb, cubed
¼ cup olive oil
1 clove garlic, chopped
3 anchovy fillets, cut into 1 in. pieces
Pinch of rosemary
½ cup sauterne or white vinegar
Salt and pepper

Brown lamb in oil over medium flame on all sides, turning occasionally. Remove meat from pan and keep it warm. Add garlic to same oil, and saute until golden brown. Add anchovies and cook until they are reduced to a paste. Add remaining ingredients to anchovies, and then return meat to the pan. Cover pan and cook over medium flame until meat is tender, about 30 minutes. Serve very hot over boiled rice or pasta, accompanied by a green salad. Serves 4 to 6.

ROASTED BABY LAMB

AGNELLINO AL FORNO

1 baby spring lamb, 7 to 8 lbs.
2 cloves garlic, slivered
½ cup lard
4 whole cloves
2 whole apples
¼ cup sauterne or water

Have butcher clean lamb thoroughly, inside and out. Wipe lamb with a damp cloth, and sprinkle with salt inside and out. Let stand for 15 minutes. Then, using a sharp knife, make 3 parallel gashes about 2½ in. long through the skin on each side of the backbone. Insert slivers of garlic into each gash. Rub the whole lamb with lard, and sprinkle with salt and pepper. Insert 2 cloves in each apple, and place inside lamb. Sew cavity with soft cord. Tie front legs forward and back legs backward, so that lamb is trussed in kneeling position. Place in an uncovered roasting pan, and roast in moderate oven 350° for 1 hour. Baste every 15 minutes with pan drippings. If lamb is too dry, add wine or water. Prick the skin several times during roasting with an icepick or fork so that it will not blister. After 1 hour turn the lamb, and raise the oven temperature to 375°. Continue to baste. Cook for another ½ hour, and turn lamb again. Cook an additional ½ hour, or until outside is dark brown and crisp. Lamb should be done in 2½ hours. To serve, place on a large board, and garnish with sprigs of parsley. Enough for 12.

NOTE: Baby lamb may also be roasted on a spit. Prepare in the same manner. Sprinkle inside and out with salt. Do not make gashes in skin, however, but instead put garlic inside body cavity with cloves and apples. Truss with wire, not cord. Roast until crisp and tender.

LAMB STEW ROMAN STYLE

ABBACHIO D'ACCIUGHI

2 lbs. stewing lamb, cubed
¼ cup oil
1 clove garlic, chopped
Salt and pepper
½ teasp. rosemary
½ teasp. sage
1 tablesp. flour
½ cup water or white wine
½ cup wine vinegar
3 anchovy fillets, chopped

Brown meat in hot oil over high flame, stirring frequently. Add garlic, salt, pepper, rosemary, sage, and flour, and stir until thoroughly blended. Brown 1 minute longer, add liquids, and stir again. Cover pan, and simmer until meat is tender, 45 minutes. Stir occasionally to prevent sticking, and if necessary add a little hot water or soup stock. One minute before meat is done add anchovies. Stir well, and correct seasonings, if necessary. Serve hot with rice or pasta. Serves 4.

STUFFED LAMB ROLL

AGNELLO RIPIENE

1 leg lamb, 3 to 4 lbs.
2 strips bacon or salt pork
½ lb. ground veal, pork, beef, or lamb
⅛ lb. prosciutto, diced
Salt and pepper
1 tablesp. shelled pine nuts
1 cup white or red wine, or water
1 piece cheesecloth large enough to cover meat

Have butcher bone leg of lamb. Combine remaining ingredients except for wine, and stuff cavity in leg. Dip cheesecloth in wine or water, and tie around leg of lamb securely. Place wrapped meat in a large kettle with water or stock to cover, add salt and pepper, and simmer covered until tender, about 2 hours. Remove meat from fire, and allow it to cool in stock. Lift meat from stock, drain, and remove cheesecloth. Chill meat, then serve on a bed of romaine, sliced into serving pieces. Serves 6 to 8.

LAMB STEW

AGNELLO IN UMIDO

1½ lbs. boneless lamb shoulder
1 clove garlic
3 tablesp. olive oil
½ small onion, chopped
½ 6-oz. can tomato paste
3 cups water
1 cup fresh shelled peas
1 medium-sized carrot, diced
Salt and pepper

Cut meat into 1½ in. cubes. Saute garlic in hot oil until golden brown. Remove garlic from pan, and add meat and onion. Brown meat evenly over medium flame; add tomato paste, water, and stir until blended. Cover pan, and cook slowly for 25 minutes. Add remaining ingredients, and cook 15 minutes longer, until both meat and vegetables are tender. Serve hot. Serves 4.

Pork

PIG'S HEAD WITH CABBAGE

TESTA DI MAIALE ALLA SICILIANA

1 pig's head
Salt and pepper
1 bay leaf
1 large onion, chopped
1 celery stalk with leaves, chopped
1 sprig parsley
1 head cabbage, quartered
6 small whole potatoes
1 6-oz. can tomato paste

Have butcher clean and crack pig's head. Scrape and wash thoroughly. Place in large kettle with cold water to cover, and add salt, pepper, onion, celery, and parsley. Simmer covered about 2½ hours, skimming occasionally. Add cabbage and peeled potatoes. Continue to cook until meat falls from bone and vegetables are tender. Serve hot in soup dish with broth. Serves 6.

PORK CHOPS FLORENTINE

COSTALLETTE ALLA FLORENTINA

1 small head red cabbage
1 tablesp. olive oil
1 onion, sliced
2 cloves garlic
4 lean pork chops, about 1½ lbs.
Salt and pepper
⅓ cup burgundy or other red wine

Quarter cabbage, and boil until tender in a small amount of salted water. Set aside. Brown onions in hot oil until soft. Remove onions and set aside. Saute garlic, pork chops, and seasonings in same oil till brown. Add wine and cooked onions, and simmer until liquid is reduced to half, about 15 minutes. Remove meat and keep warm.

Squeeze cooked cabbage dry with hands, and add to sauce. Let sauce come to a boil, and place chops on top of cabbage. Cover and cook slowly over low flame 10 minutes, until chops are thoroughly re-heated. Chops should be served hot on top of cabbage. Serves 4.

PORK CHOPS WITH MARSALA

COSTATELLE DI MAIALE CON MARSALA

1 cup bread crumbs
6 tablesp. grated Parmesan or Romano cheese
Salt and pepper
1 tablesp. chopped parsley
2 eggs, slightly beaten
4 loin pork chops
1 cup diced celery
2 small onions, sliced
½ cup marsala

Combine crumbs, cheese, seasonings, and parsley. Dip pork chops in slightly beaten eggs, then roll in crumb mixture. Fry chops in a small amount of oil until well browned on both sides. Drain excess fat from pan, arrange chops in bottom of pan, and put the diced celery and sliced onions on top of them. Sprinkle lightly with salt and pepper, and add marsala. Cover pan and cook over low flame until meat is tender and well done, about 25 minutes. Serve hot, with gravy. Serves 4. VARIATION: Use veal chops instead of pork shops, if desired. Wine may be replaced by water.

PORK CHOPS NEAPOLITAN STYLE

COSTATELLE DI MAIALE ALLA NAPOLITANA

6 loin pork chops, ½ in. thick
½ cup salad oil
1 qt. button mushrooms
1 sweet green pepper, cut in eighths
1 large onion, sliced
1 #2 can tomatoes
Salt and pepper

Brown chops in oil over high flame on both sides. Remove from pan and transfer to large saucepan. Saute mushrooms and peppers in same oil as chops over medium flame until soft. Add to chops. Fry onion in same oil until soft, add tomatoes, and simmer 5 minutes. Pour this sauce over chops, season with salt and pepper, cover pan, and cook slowly over low flame until chops and vegetables are tender, about 30 minutes. Serve hot. Serves 6.

PICKLED PORK CHOPS

COSTATELLE DI MAIALE AL ACETO

6 loin pork chops, about 1½ lbs.
1 cup wine vinegar
2 cloves garlic, chopped
½ teasp. fennel seeds
3 tablesp. olive oil
Salt and pepper

Combine vinegar, garlic, and fennel seed, and marinate chops in this mixture for 1 hour. Drain and wipe dry. Sprinkle chops with salt and pepper, and saute in oil over medium flame until tender and well done, about 15 to 20 minutes. Serve hot. Serves 6.

ROAST PORK TUSCANY

MAIALE FORNO ALLA TUSCAN

4 or 5 lbs. pork loin
2 cloves garlic, slivered
2 sprigs fresh rosemary, or 1 teasp. dried rosemary
Salt and pepper

Have butcher make a few incisions in pork, and insert garlic slivers into cuts. Rub meat with garlic and rosemary, sprinkle with salt and pepper, and roast in an uncovered roasting pan in a hot oven 450° 10 to 15 minutes. Reduce heat to 350° and roast 1½ to 1¾ hours, basting frequently with pan drippings. *Be sure pork is well done, and that the juice is not pink.* Remove pork from oven, cool to room temperature, slice, and serve with browned fried potatoes and vegetables. Serves 6.

SPARERIBS WITH POTATOES

COSTOLE DI MAIALE CON PATATE

1 set spareribs, ½ to 2 lbs.
1 tablesp salad oil
1 clove garlic
1 6-oz. can tomato puree
2 cups water
3 medium-sized potatoes, quartered
Salt and pepper

Cut spareribs into serving pieces, and brown in oil on both sides over medium flame. Transfer to another saucepan. Fry garlic in same oil until golden brown, remove garlic, and pour tomato puree and water into pan. Stir until well blended, and then pour over spareribs. Cover pan and simmer 30 minutes. Add quartered potatoes and seasonings. Cover and cook until meat and potatoes are tender, adding more water if necessary. Serve hot. Serves 4.

ROAST SUCKLING PIG

MAIALINO ARROSTITO

1 suckling pig, about 10 lbs. Pig should not be more than 5 to 6 weeks old
2 teasp. dried or fresh rosemary
3 cloves garlic
⅓ cup salad oil or lard
Salt and pepper
Juice of 1 lemon

Have butcher clean and draw pig. Wipe it with a damp cloth inside and out. Using a sharp knife, make 3 parallel gashes about 2½ in. long on either side of the backbone. Insert 1 clove of garlic and a little rosemary into each cut. Brush the outside of the pig with oil, and sprinkle with salt and pepper inside and out. Rub lemon juice inside of pig. Truss pig so that it is in a kneeling position, using soft cord. Roast uncovered in 325° oven, basting every 10 minutes or so with pan drippings. Prick the skin several times during cooking so that it will not blister. Cook until tender, 3 to 3½ hours. Place on a board, dress with raw eating apples or vegetables, cut into serving slices, and serve hot. Serves 8 to 10.
NOTE: The pig may be roasted on a spit. Prepare the same way, truss well with wire, and roast, allowing 35 minutes per pound.

Rabbit

FRIED RABBIT WITH SAUTERNE

CONIGLIO CON SAUTERNE

1 rabbit, about 3 lbs.
2 tablesp. salt
½ cup olive oil
Pinch of rosemary
Salt and pepper
1 cup sauterne

Cut rabbit into 8 pieces, and soak in salted cold water to cover for 3 hours. Wash and wipe dry. Fry rabbit in hot oil 5 minutes, until brown. Add rosemary, salt, pepper, and wine. Cover pan, reduce heat to low, and cook until rabbit is tender, about 1 hour. Serve hot, with pan juices. Serves 4.

RABBIT STEW

CONIGLIO STUFATO

1 rabbit, about 3 lbs.
2 tablesp. salt
2 tablesp. olive oil
2 strips salt pork, diced
1 medium-sized onion, chopped
1 clove garlic, minced
2 tablesp. minced parsley
1 cup Italian red wine
½ bay leaf
Salt and pepper

Cut rabbit into 8 pieces, and soak in salted cold water to cover for 3 hours. Wash and wipe dry. Saute rabbit, oil, salt pork, onion, and garlic in saucepan until well browned on all sides, about 30 minutes. Add parsley, wine, bay leaf, and seasonings. Cover pan and cook over low fire until rabbit is tender, about ½ hour. Serve hot. Serves 4.

RABBIT SWEET AND SOUR

CONIGLIO DOLCE E AGRO

1 rabbit, 3 to 4 lbs.
2 tablesp. salt
4 tablesp. olive oil
1 #2 can tomatoes
2 tablesp. olive oil
2 medium-sized onions, diced
¼ lb. green pitted olives
1 tablesp. capers
½ cup wine vinegar
½ cup water
2 teasp. sugar
Salt and pepper

Cut rabbit into 8 pieces, and soak in salted water to cover for 3 hours. Wash and wipe dry. Saute rabbit in 4 tablesp. oil until brown on all sides. Add tomatoes, and simmer covered for 15 minutes. Heat 2 tablesp. oil in a separate pan. Add onions and saute until soft. Add olives, capers, vinegar, water, and sugar, and cook for 3 minutes. Pour sauce over rabbit, season with salt and pepper, and cook slowly in covered pan until rabbit is tender, about 20 minutes. Serve hot with sauce. Serves 4.

VENISON STEAK

BISTECCA DI CERVO

1 venison steak, 1 in. thick, about 1½ lbs.
½ cup olive oil
¼ cup burgundy
1 clove garlic, minced
Pinch of marjoram
Salt and pepper

Marinate steak in mixture of olive oil, wine, garlic and marjoram for 10 minutes. Pat dry with soft cloth, and broil on preheated broiler 4 in. from fire, about 5 minutes on each side. (Venison should be served rare.) Sprinkle with salt and pepper, and serve immediately. Serves 2.

Italian Sausages

There are 2 kinds of Italian fresh sausages, sweet and hot. They may be used interchangeably, depending on your personal taste.

HINTS FOR PREPARING ITALIAN SAUSAGES

1. Do not add seasoning, as there is enough in the sausage already.

2. Prick sausage with a fork during cooking.
3. Remove string either before or after cooking.
4. The easiest way to handle a sausage in a flat or shallow pan is to put one end of the sausage in the center of the pan and wrap the rest around it in a circle.

ROASTED SAUSAGE

SALSICCIA ARROSTITI

2 lbs. Italian sweet or hot sausage
¼ cup red wine

Place sausage in shallow pan, and pour wine over it. Bake in moderate 350° oven 20 to 30 minutes. Sausage should be golden brown on the outside and gray on the inside. IF THE SAUSAGE IS PINK ON THE INSIDE, IT IS NOT DONE. Prick sausage with fork 10 minutes after placing in oven. Serve hot. Serves 6.

OMELET PEASANT STYLE: *See p. 135.*

SAUSAGE WITH GREEN PEPPERS

SALSICCIA CON PEPPERONI

1½ lbs. Italian sweet or hot sausage
4 green peppers
Loaf of Italian bread

Place sausage in cold frying pan, and fry over medium flame, uncovered, for 20 minutes. Prick during frying, and turn frequently. Wash pepper, removing seeds, stem, and pith. Cut into quarters, add to sausage, and cook, covered, until sausage is done, about 10 minutes more.

Cut bread into 3 in. slices, and place piece of sausage on each slice. Cover with peppers, and spoon 1 teasp. pan drippings over each serving. Serve very hot. Serves 6.

POLENTA WITH SAUSAGE: *See p. 155.*

CHAPTER SEVEN

Fish

MARINATED FISH

MARINATE PESCE

2 lbs. mackerel, sardines, porgies, sea bass, sole, snapper, red mullet, or jumbo shrimp
1 onion, sliced
2 tablesp. chopped parsley
1 bay leaf, crushed
Pinch of rosemary or oregano
Juice of 2 lemons
Enough white wine to cover fish, about 1½ cups

If using whole fish, remove heads, tails, and split in half. Remove bones. If using shrimp, shell and de-vein.

Place cleaned fish in saucepan, and add sliced onion, parsley, bay leaf, rosemary, lemon juice, and wine. Season with salt and pepper. Simmer over low fire 6 minutes. Cool in marinade, and refrigerate overnight. Next day remove fish from marinade gently with a pancake turner or slotted spoon, and place in a deep dish. Strain marinade, and pour it over fish. The fish may be served cold as a main dish, or as antipasto. Serves 6.

CHARCOAL GRILLED BASS

RAGNO ALLA GRIGLIA

2 bass, 1½ lbs. each
½ cup olive oil
Salt and pepper
Juice of 2 lemons
2 tablesp. chopped parsley or fresh mint
1 clove garlic chopped fine (optional)

Have fish dealer clean fish, leaving heads and tails on. Make 2½ in. slits across the body on both sides about ¼ in. deep. Wash fish thoroughly, and dry on absorbent paper. Blend oil, salt, and pepper, and brush both sides of fish with this mixture. Grill over low charcoal fire about 6 in. from flame, allowing about 15 minutes for each side. Turn 2 or 3 times during cooking, and brush with more oil, if necessary. Remove from grill, place on serving dish, and pour combined lemon juice, parsley or mint, and garlic over fish. Serves 4.
NOTE: Freshly caught trout and mackerel may also be prepared in this manner. Grill 10 minutes on each side, and serve immediately.

BAKED CODFISH

BACCALA AL FORNO

1 whole dry codfish, about 2 lbs.
½ cup olive oil
3 tablesp. raisins
1 tablesp. chopped celery
1 tablesp. oregano
3 tablesp. grated Parmesan cheese
1½ cups bread crumbs
1 clove garlic, minced
1 tablesp. minced parsley
3 medium-sized potatoes, sliced ½ in. thick
½ cup water
Pepper

Soak fish in cold water 2 days, changing water four times. Drain and cut into serving pieces. Pour half the olive oil in bottom of baking pan, and place a layer of codfish in it. Combine raisins, celery, oregano, cheese, crumbs, garlic, and parsley, and sprinkle about half this mixture over the fish. Put a layer of sliced potatoes on top of crumbs. Repeat these layers until all ingredients are used, reserving some crumbs for a top layer. Pour water over all, and add ¼ cup olive oil. Sprinkle with pepper, and bake in moderate oven 375° until potatoes are tender, about 30 minutes. Serve immediately. Serves 6 to 8.

CODFISH CROQUETTES

BACCALA CROCHE

1 lb. salted codfish
1 cup bread crumbs
1 tablesp. minced parsley
1 egg
1 tablesp. grated Romano cheese
1 small onion, chopped
¾ cup olive oil
Pepper

Soak fish in cold water to cover for 2 days, during which time change water four times. Drain and cut cod in 3 pieces. Place in sauce pan with 2 qts. cold water, and simmer for 30 minutes. Cool and drain. Remove skin and bones, and shred meat. Add crumbs, parsley, egg, cheese, onion, and pepper. Taste to see if any salt is needed. Mix thoroughly and shape into 2 in. croquettes. Fry croquettes in hot oil over medium flame 4 minutes on each side, until golden brown. Drain on absorbent paper, garnish with lemon wedges, and serve at once. Serves 4.

CONCHES

SCUNGILLI

Conches are big sea snails, about 3 in. in diameter. The meat has a sweet taste similar to scallops. Conches are usually cooked for salads, but they may also be served cooked in a sauce and eaten from the shells. The following recipe is for the conch salad traditionally served by the Italian people for Christmas and New Year's Eve dinners.

4 large conches
1 clove garlic, chopped
¼ cup olive oil
Juice of 1 lemon; or, 3 tablesp. wine vinegar
Salt and pepper
1 tablesp. chopped parsley
Pinch of oregano (optional)

Select fresh conches and scrub with a vegetable brush in tepid water until all sand is removed. Place in a large kettle and cover with briskly boiling water. Cover pan tightly, and cook slowly over a low flame for 1 hour, until half the body of the conch protrudes from the shell. Remove from heat and run cold water into pan. Take meat out of shells with fork. Cut off hard outer cover. Cut meat into ½ in. slices, and cover with dressing made from remaining ingredients. Toss with two forks until meat is well covered with dressing. Serve hot or cold. Serves 6.

CRABS

GRANCHI

1 dozen live crabs
1½ teasp. salt
1 teasp. caraway seeds (optional)

Wash crabs. Bring about 3 qts. salted water to a rolling boil, and drop crabs into water 1 at a time, head first. Add caraway seeds. Cover pan, and cook crabs over low fire 20 minutes until shells are red and flesh is white. Remove from heat and run just enough cold water into the pan so that the crabs can be handled. Serve immediately, with any desired sauce. Basic Tomato Sauce, p. 61, is very good.

EELS FLORENTINE STYLE

ANGUILLE ALLA FIORENTINA

2 lbs. long eels
½ cup olive oil
1 clove garlic, chopped
2 pieces bay leaf
1 cup bread crumbs
Salt and pepper
2 tablesp. white wine

Skin and wash eels. Cut into 2½ in. pieces. Mix oil, garlic, and bay leaf, and heat slightly. Place crumbs in a bowl, and season with salt and pepper. Roll eels in hot oil, then in seasoned crumbs, and then place in baking dish. Add remainder of oil, and wine, and bake in moderate oven 375° until tender, about ½ hour. Turn gently a few times during baking. Serve hot. Serves 4.

MARINATED EEL

ANGUILLE MARINATE

1½ lbs. large eels, cleaned and split
6 tablesp. olive oil
1 clove garlic, chopped
Pinch of oregano
1 bay leaf
1 cup wine vinegar
¼ cup water
Salt and pepper

Wash eels and cut into 1½ in. pieces. Fry in oil over medium heat for 6 to 8 minutes, until tender. Transfer to a deep bowl and cool. Simmer garlic, oregano, bay leaf, vinegar, water, salt and pepper for 8 minutes. Cool and pour over cooked eels. Store in refrigerator until needed. Serves 4. This will keep for a week in the refrigerator, and the longer the eels are marinated, the better the flavor will be.

EEL STEW ROMAN STYLE

CAPITONE ALLA ROMANA

1 small eel, about 1 lb.
4 tablesp. olive oil
1 medium-sized onion, sliced
1 cup canned strained tomatoes
1 cup fresh shelled peas
Salt and pepper
1 tablesp. chopped parsley
½ cup white wine (optional)

Have eel's head removed, and have eel cleaned. Wash, and cut into 3 in. pieces crosswise. Brown onion lightly in oil, and add strained tomatoes, eel, and shelled peas. Season with salt and pepper, add parsley and wine, and cook over medium heat until eel is tender, about 15 minutes. Serve hot. Serves 4.

FROGS' LEGS

RANOCCHIE

1 dozen frogs' legs
1 cup bread crumbs
Salt and pepper
2 eggs, slightly beaten
1 cup salad oil
3 sprigs parsley
4 lemon wedges

Wash frogs' legs in cold water. Combine crumbs and seasonings, and roll frogs' legs in crumbs. Dip them in slightly beaten eggs, and then roll in crumbs again. Saute frogs' legs in oil until golden brown on both sides, about 5 minutes. Garnish with parsley and lemon wedges, and serve immediately. Serves 4.

BAKED HADDOCK

PESCE BIANCO AL FORNO

1 haddock or lake trout, 3 to 4 lbs.
1 tablesp. minced parsley
2 tablesp. chopped onion
1 tablesp. oregano
6 tablesp. olive oil
Salt and pepper
1 #2 can tomatoes

Have fish thoroughly cleaned. Cut 3 crosswise gashes in front and back of fish about 1½ in. long. Stuff each gash with parsley and onion. Place fish in greased baking pan, using ¼ cup olive oil. Sprinkle with salt, pepper, and oregano. Dribble 2 additional tablesp. oil over fish. Mash tomatoes with a fork, and pour them over fish. Bake in hot oven 425° 10 minutes. Reduce heat to 400° and bake until tender, about ½ hour. Serve hot. Serves 6.

DEVILED LOBSTER

ARAGOSTA FRA DIAVOLO

1 large live lobster, about 2½ lbs.
3 tablesp. olive oil
1 clove garlic, minced
1 #2 can tomatoes; or, 1 #2 can tomato puree
1 tablesp. minced parsley
1 tablesp. oregano
Pinch of red pepper (optional)
Salt and pepper

Split lobster lengthwise. Clean by removing sac behind head and the dark vein which runs the length of the tail. Leave the green part (liver) in the lobster. Place the cleaned lobster in a shallow baking dish. Brown garlic in oil 1 minute, add tomato puree or canned tomatoes, parsley, oregano, red pepper, and salt and pepper, and cook over low flame 10 minutes. Pour hot sauce over uncooked lobster, making certain that lobster is well covered with sauce. Bake in moderate oven 350° 18 to 20 minutes. *Do not overcook,* or lobster will be tough. Serve immediately. Serves 2.

LOBSTER SALAD

INSALATA ARAGOSTA

1 clove garlic
6 tablesp. olive oil
3 tablesp. wine vinegar
Pinch of oregano
Salt and pepper
1 live lobster, about 1½ lbs.

Combine garlic, olive oil, vinegar, and oregano, and set aside. Bring 4 qts. salted water to a rolling boil, and plunge lobster into it head first. Cover pan and cook over medium flame 15 to 20 minutes. Remove lobster from water, and drain or wipe dry. Split lobster lengthwise, and clean by removing sac behind head and dark vein which runs the length of tail.

Leave the green part (liver). Twist the claws, and crack them with a pair of pliers. Remove meat from lobster, cut into large pieces, place it in a serving bowl, and pour previously prepared dressing over it. Season with salt and pepper. Mix thoroughly, and serve cold on crisp romaine. Serves 2 to 3.

LOBSTER IN WINE SAUCE

ARAGOSTA CON SALSA DI VINO

1 live lobster, about 1½ lbs.
½ cup olive oil
Salt and pepper
½ cup sherry
2 tablesp. brandy

Bring 4 qts. salted water to a rolling boil, and plunge live lobster into it head first. Cover pan, and cook over medium flame 15 to 20 minutes. Drain and wipe dry. Split lobster lengthwise, and clean by removing sac behind head and dark vein which runs the length of tail. Leave green part (liver) in lobster. Twist the claws and crack them with a pair of pliers. Remove lobster meat and cut into serving pieces. Pour oil into a large frying pan, and add lobster meat. Simmer for 3 minutes, and season with salt and pepper. Add sherry and brandy, and cook 2 minutes longer. *Do not allow to boil.* Serve immediately. Serves 2.

MUSSELS MARINER STYLE

MITILI MARINARA

2 doz. mussels, in shells
¼ cup olive oil
1 clove garlic
2 tablesp. tomato paste
½ cup water
Salt and pepper
2 cups cooked rice
1 tablesp. minced parsley

Select fresh mussels with tightly closed shells. Scrub well with vegetable brush, and scrape off hairy beard with a knife. Rinse well under cold water. Brown garlic in hot oil 2 minutes. Add tomato paste, water, and seasonings, and blend well. Add mussels. Cover pan and cook over low flame 10 to 20 minutes, until shells open. Serve the hot mussels over cooked rice, and sprinkle with minced parsley. Serves 4.
NOTE: Clams may be used in this recipe, also. Follow directions given, cooking until shells open. Either mussels or clams may be served over toast instead of rice.

OCTOPUS SALAD

INSALATA DI POLPO

1 fresh octopus, about 2 lbs.
4 qts. water
2 tablesp. salt
¼ cup wine vinegar; or, juice of 2 lemons
1 teasp. olive oil (optional)
Salt and pepper

Have fish dealer remove octopus eyes and mouth. Wash octopus by running cold water over it for ½ hour. Pour 4 qts. cold water into a large kettle, add salt, and bring to a rolling boil. Pierce neck of octopus with a large fork. Then, holding the neck out of water with the fork, dip the tentacles into the briskly boiling salted water three times. The third time slide the octopus off the fork, and leave it in the water. Cook uncovered until tender, about ½ hour. Do not overcook. Drain octopus in large colander, and allow to cool to room temperature. Cut meat into 2 in. pieces, and combine with remaining ingredients. Toss well with a wooden spoon and fork. Serve with Italian red wine. Serves 6. It will keep for about a week, under refrigeration.
NOTE: Octopus can be purchased at any Italian fish market. Its meat is similar to squid, with a rich, sweet flavor. The above salad is traditionally served on Christmas Eve.

OCTOPUS WITH TOMATO SAUCE

POLPO CON SALSA

1 fresh octopus, about 1½ lbs.
4 tablesp. olive oil
1 clove garlic
½ cup sherry
1 #2 can tomatoes
Salt and pepper

Have octopus skinned, cleaned, and cut into 2 in. pieces. The octopus ink may be removed, or left on. If it is left on, the sauce will have a richer flavor. Brown garlic in oil until golden brown, and then add octopus. Cover and saute over a low flame 10 minutes. Add wine, and continue cooking 10 minutes longer. Add tomatoes and seasonings. Cover and cook until tender, turning occasionally, about 15 minutes. Serve hot. Serves 6.

BAKED OYSTERS

OSTRICHE ALLA FORNO

2 doz. large oysters in shells
¼ cup olive oil
1 tablesp. chopped parsley
1 clove garlic, chopped
1 cup bread crumbs
2 tablesp. grated Parmesan cheese
¼ teasp. salt
Pinch of cayenne pepper
Lemon wedges

Scrub oyster shells thoroughly. Wash 1 at a time in ½ cup cold water, and pry shells open by inserting a thin-bladed knife around the edges of the shell and prying upwards. Discard flat shell.

Combine remaining ingredients, and mix well. Carefully place oysters in a baking pan, making sure that they lie flat, so you will not lose any of the juice. Sprinkle about ½ teasp. crumb mixture over each oyster, and bake in moderate oven 350° 10 minutes. Serve immediately, garnished with lemon wedges. Serves 4.

POMPANO

FILETTI DI POMPANO

2 pompanos, about 1½ lbs. each
3 tablesp. butter
Salt and pepper
½ cup sauterne or any white wine
2 tablesp. minced parsley
4 lemon wedges

Have fish boned, split, and filleted into 8 fillets. Wash and wipe dry. Grease a shallow baking pan with 1 tablesp. butter, lay fillets in pan, and sprinkle with salt and pepper. Dot with balance of butter, and put on pre-heated broiler 4 in. from flame. When butter begins to melt, baste with wine. Broil fish about 5 minutes, turn, baste again, and broil 7 minutes more until fish breaks easily into flakes when tested with a fork. Do not overcook. Serve on a hot platter garnished with lemon wedges and parsley. Serves 4.

ROSEFISH PALERMO STYLE

PESCE ROSSO ALLA PALERMITANA

1 rosefish, about 2 lbs.
2 cups water
Salt and pepper
1 tablesp. chopped parsley
3 tablesp. olive oil
1 small onion, chopped fine
4 slices buttered toast

Have fish cleaned and filleted. Keep backbone and head. Put fillets through food chopper, using medium blade. Boil water, salt, and pepper, and add chopped fish and parsley. Add head and backbone. Cook over medium flame 10 minutes, remove head and backbone, and strain broth. Keep broth warm. Brown onion lightly, add chopped fish which has been strained from broth, and cook until well browned, about 7 minutes. When brown, spread chopped fish on buttered toast

slices, pour ¼ cup hot broth over each portion, and serve immediately. Serves 4. An excellent dish for Lent.
NOTE: Rosefish are also called sea perch, bright eye, and red fish.

BAKED SALMON STEAK WITH WINE SAUCE

SALMONE AL FORNO CON SALSA DI VINO

2 lbs. fresh salmon slices, ½ in. thick
Salt and pepper
1 cup sherry
1 clove garlic, chopped (optional)
¼ cup olive oil
Juice of 1 lemon

Place salmon slices in baking pan, and sprinkle with salt and pepper. Combine remaining ingredients, and pour over fish. Bake until tender in hot oven 400°, about ½ hour. Do not overcook. Serve immediately. Serves 6.

STUFFED SARDINES

SARDE IMBOTTITE

1½ lbs. fresh sardines
1 cup bread crumbs
1 clove garlic, chopped
3 tablesp. olive oil
1 teasp. chopped parsley
1 tablesp. white raisins
Salt and pepper
2 tablesp. olive oil
1 #2½ can tomatoes, strained

Have fish dealer clean sardines, cut off heads, and remove bones, leaving fish whole. Stuff fish ⅔ full with stuffing made by combining crumbs, garlic, oil, parsley, raisins, salt, and pepper. Tie fish closed with soft white string. Grease bottom of baking dish with 2 tablesp. olive oil, place fish in pan, and pour tomatoes on top of them. Bake in hot oven 400° until tender, about ½ hour. Remove fish from pan with a pancake

turner, place on hot platter, and remove string. Spoon sauce from pan over fish, and serve immediately. Serves 4.
NOTE: This dish may also be prepared on top of the stove. Place stuffed fish in large frying pan, pour strained tomatoes over them, cover, and simmer for 15 minutes, or until tender.

SCALLOPS VENETIAN STYLE

CONCHIGLIA ALLA VENEZIA

2 lbs. scallops
2 eggs, well beaten
1 cup bread crumbs
3 tablesp. grated Parmesan cheese
Pinch of marjoram
2 cups salad oil
6 lemon wedges
Salt and pepper

Dip scallops in beaten eggs, then roll in mixture of bread crumbs, cheese, salt, pepper, and marjoram. Fry scallops in hot oil over medium flame until brown on both sides. Serve hot garnished with lemon wedges. Enough for 6.

SHRIMP AND RICE RAGOUT

RISOTTA ALLA CERTOSINA

¼ cup olive oil
1 large onion, minced
1 celery stalk, minced
1 #2 can tomatoes
Salt and pepper
½ cup fresh mushrooms, sliced
2 cups cooked green peas
2 cups cooked and cleaned shrimp; or, 2 cups cooked lobster meat
2 cups cooked rice

Saute onion and celery in oil until celery is soft. Stir occasionally. Add tomatoes, and seasoning, and bring to a boil. Reduce heat and simmer 20 minutes, stirring occasionally.

Add mushrooms and cook 5 minutes, then add peas and shrimp or lobster. Continue cooking until all ingredients are thoroughly hot, then pour over rice and serve immediately. Serves 4.

MARY'S FRIED SHRIMP

GAMBERI FRITTI ALLA MARIA

2 lbs. jumbo shrimp
2 eggs, slightly beaten
⅓ cup grated Parmesan cheese
1 cup bread crumbs
Salt and pepper
2 cups olive or salad oil

Shell and de-vein shrimp. Roll them in beaten eggs, in bread crumbs, and in cheese. Season with salt and pepper. Fry shrimps in hot oil until brown on both sides, about 5 minutes. Drain on unglazed paper, and serve hot or cold. Serves 3 to 4.

FRIED SKATE

PESCE INDORATO E FRITTO

2 lbs. skate slices, 1 in. thick
1 cup peanut or salad oil
1 cup flour
Salt and pepper
3 tablesp. chopped parsley
Juice of 1 lemon

Cut skate into serving pieces. Combine flour, salt, and pepper, and roll fish in this mixture. Then fry in oil over high fire until golden brown on both sides, about 6 minutes. Transfer to hot platter, sprinkle with parsley, and pour lemon juice over fish. Serve very hot. Serves 6.

BOILED SNAILS

CHIOCCIOLE

2 lbs. live snails
1 tablesp. salt

Put snails in large pot, cover with water, and add salt. Let stand 3 hours. Rinse thoroughly several times with fresh water, and drain well. Cover snails with fresh water, cover pot, and cook over low flame until snails protrude half-way out of shells. Then turn heat up to medium flame, and cook about ½ hour. Remove pan from fire, and let snails cool in water. Serve in shells, and use a small oyster fork or nut pick to extract meat. Serves 2.

SNAILS PALERMO STYLE

CHIOCCIOLE ALLA PALERMITANA

2 lbs. live snails
3 tablesp. olive oil
2 cloves garlic, chopped; or 1 small onion, chopped
1 6-oz. can tomato paste
2½ cups water
Salt and pepper

Cover snails with cold water, add 1 tablesp. salt, and let stand for 3 hours. Rinse thoroughly several times with fresh water, and drain well.

Brown garlic or onion in oil for 2 minutes, add tomato paste and water, and stir until well blended. Simmer uncovered for 15 minutes. Add snails and seasonings. Continue to simmer 20 minutes, stirring occasionally. Remove snails from sauce with a slotted spoon and put in serving dish. Spoon some sauce over snails, and pour rest of sauce over ½ lb. cooked pasta. Serves 4.

FILLET OF SOLE GENOA STYLE

SOGLIOLE ALLA GENOVESE

1½ lbs. fillet of sole
5 tablesp. olive oil
1 cup water, fish stock, or tomato juice
¾ cup bread crumbs
1 tablesp. oregano
2 sprigs parsley, minced
Salt and pepper
Juice of ½ lemon

Clean and wash fish. Grease a baking dish with oil, and lay fillets in the bottom of the greased dish. Pour liquid around them. Combine remaining ingredients except lemon juice, and sprinkle over fish. Bake in a moderate oven 350° until fish flakes easily, about 15 minutes. Do not overcook. Sprinkle fillets with lemon juice and serve immediately. Serves 4.

SQUID WITH ONIONS

CALAMAI CON CIPOLLE

2 lbs. fresh squid
2 large onions, sliced
½ cup olive oil
½ cup water
Salt and pepper

Have fish dealer clean squid thoroughly, removing eyes, outside skin, and intestines. Wash under running cold water, and cut off head and tentacles. Cut squid into 2 in. rings. Brown onions in oil, add cut-up squid, water, and seasonings. Cover and simmer over medium flame until tender, about 20 minutes. Stir occasionally. Serve hot. Serves 6.

STUFFED SQUID

CALAMAI IMBOTTITI

8 small squid
1 small onion, chopped
2 tablesp. raisins
1½ cups bread crumbs
1 teasp. minced parsley
2 tablesp. grated Parmesan cheese
Salt and pepper
1 egg, well beaten

Have fish dealer clean squid thoroughly, removing eyes, outside skin, and intestines. Cut off heads and tentacles. Wash well, and drain.

Combine remaining ingredients, and fill the cavity in each squid with stuffing. Sew squid closed, or fasten with toothpicks. Place in baking pan, and cover with the following sauce:

1 #2 can tomatoes *4 tablesp. olive oil*
1 clove garlic

Brown garlic in oil, mash tomatoes with fork, and add. Simmer for 10 minutes. Then pour over squid, and bake in hot oven 400° for 35 minutes, or until tender. Serve whole with sauce. Serves 8.

SQUID WITH WINE

CALAMAI CON VINO

1 lb. squid
2 tablesp. olive oil
1 clove garlic
¼ cup Italian red wine
Salt and pepper
1 tablesp. chopped parsley

Clean squid thoroughly, removing outside skin, intestines, and eyes. Wash well under cold running water, cut off heads and tentacles, and chop these into small pieces. Cut body into 2 in. rings. Brown garlic in oil over medium flame, add squid, and saute 3 minutes, turning frequently. Add wine, salt, pepper, and parsley, cover pan, and simmer until tender, about 10 minutes. Serve hot over cooked rice or buttered toast. Serves 3 or 4.

BROILED SWORDFISH

PESCE SPADA ALLA GRIGLIA

2 lbs. swordfish
5 tablesp. olive oil
Salt and pepper
6 lemon wedges

Wipe fish with damp cloth. Brush with oil, and place in a shallow baking pan. Sprinkle with salt and pepper, and broil 2 in. from fire 15 minutes. Turn and broil 5 minutes longer.

Add more oil if fish gets dry. Transfer to a hot platter and serve immediately, garnished with lemon wedges. Serves 6. NOTE: Do not try to broil less than 2 lbs. of swordfish, as it will get too dry.

MARINATED SWORDFISH

PESCE SPADA MARINATO

2 lbs. swordfish
1 cup olive oil
½ clove garlic
2 sprigs of parsley, minced; or, 2 sprigs fresh mint, minced
2 scallions, minced
1 teasp. oregano
Salt and pepper
1½ cups bread crumbs
1 cup grated Parmesan cheese

Have fish sliced 1 in. thick. Combine oil, garlic, parsley, scallions, oregano, salt, and pepper, and marinate fish in this for 2 hours. Drain oil off marinade, and reserve 3 tablesp. Combine bread crumbs and cheese, and dip fish in crumbs. Pour reserved olive oil in baking dish, put fish in dish, and bake in a moderate oven 350° until tender, 30 to 40 minutes. Serve hot. Serves 6.

BROILED TROUT

TROTA ALLA GRIGLIA

2 lbs. trout
4 tablesp. olive oil
1 teasp. minced parsley
Juice of 2 lemons
Salt and pepper

Have fish dealer clean trout and remove head. Combine oil, parsley, lemon juice and seasonings, and brush fish with this mixture, reserving some part of it. Place trout flesh side up on a preheated broiler 3 in. from flame, and broil 6 minutes. Turn, brush with reserved oil, and broil 6 more minutes, until skin is brown and crisp, and flesh is tender. Place on a hot platter, spoon sauce from pan over it, and serve immediately. Serves 4.

TUNA WITH GREEN OLIVES

TONNO CON OLIVE VERDE

2 lbs. fresh tuna
½ cup olive oil
2 large onions, sliced
½ lb. green Italian olives, pitted
½ cup wine vinegar
1½ teasp. sugar
Salt and pepper

Wipe fish with damp cloth, and sprinkle with salt and pepper. Saute fish in oil over medium flame until brown on both sides, about 8 minutes. Remove fish from pan, and set aside. Saute onions in same oil 3 minutes. Add olives, and cook 2 minutes more. Add vinegar and sugar, and simmer over low flame for 5 minutes. Place fish in sauce, cover pan, and simmer for 5 minutes. Serve either hot or cold. Serves 4. This will keep well in the refrigerator for 2 or 3 days.

TUNA SALAD

INSALATA DI TONNO

1 lb. fresh tuna
1 clove garlic, chopped
¼ cup lemon juice
3 tablesp. olive oil
2 tablesp. fresh basil
Salt and pepper

Simmer fish in 2 cups salted water until tender, about 30 minutes. Drain and cool. Break meat into small pieces with a fork. Blend remaining ingredients and pour over fish. Toss lightly, and serve. Serves 6. This fish will keep for a week in the refrigerator. It is an excellent antipasto.

TUNA HUNTER'S STYLE

TONNO ALLA CACCIATORA

2 lbs. fresh tuna
2 medium-sized onions, sliced
½ cup olive oil
5 hot yellow peppers; or,
4 green peppers
8 fresh tomatoes
¼ cup fresh basil, chopped
Salt and pepper

Wipe tuna with damp cloth. Saute onions in oil until soft over medium flame. Remove and set aside. Saute the tuna in the same oil until browned on both sides. Remove and set aside. Wash peppers, and remove stems, seeds, and pith. Cut yellow peppers in half lengthwise or cut green peppers into quarters. Saute 3 minutes in same oil, adding a little if necessary. Peel tomatoes, cut them in small pieces, and add to peppers. Add basil, cover, and simmer 10 minutes, stirring frequently. Add cooked onions to sauce. Place tuna in sauce, season with salt and pepper, cover pan, and simmer till tuna is done, about 5 minutes more. Serve hot or cold. Serves 6. Tuna prepared this way may be stored for a week in the refrigerator.

WHITING WITH TOMATO SAUCE

MERLUZZO CON POMODORO SALSA

2 lbs. whiting, cleaned and dressed
3 tablesp. olive oil
1 small onion, chopped
½ clove garlic
1 #2½ can Italian plum tomatoes
Salt and pepper
1 tablesp. chopped parsley
2 tablesp. Italian red wine

Saute onion and garlic in oil until browned. Mash tomatoes with fork, and add to pan. Add salt, pepper, and parsley, and simmer, covered, 25 minutes, stirring occasionally. Add whiting to sauce and cook 8 minutes longer. Add wine and continue cooking until fish is tender, about 2 or 3 minutes more. Do not overcook. Serve either as a main dish, or as a sauce for pasta. Enough for ½ lb. pasta. Serves 6.

VARIATIONS: 1. Substitute 1½ lbs. fillet of sole for whiting.

2. 1½ lbs. codfish may be used instead of whiting. Soak fish, and prepare in same manner, adding ¼ lb. green Italian olives pitted and chopped to sauce.
3. Use 1½ lbs. tuna fish instead of whiting. Make 2 slits 1 in. long on either side of fish slices, and stuff with 1 minced clove garlic combined with 2 tablesp. grated Romano cheese and 1 tablesp. chopped parsley or basil. Simmer tuna fish 15 minutes in partially cooked sauce, and serve as directed.

CHAPTER EIGHT

Poultry

CHICKEN AGRIGENTO

POLLO ALLA AGRIGENTO

1 chicken, 3 to 3½ lbs.
Salt and pepper
¼ cup olive oil
3 medium-sized onions, chopped
*¼ cup fresh or dried mushrooms**
1 cup canned tomatoes
½ teasp. fennel, seeds or ground
¼ cup sherry

Have butcher cut chicken into serving pieces. Wash and wipe dry, and sprinkle with salt and pepper. Saute chicken in hot oil over medium flame until light brown on all sides. Reduce heat to low, add rest of ingredients, and simmer in tightly covered pan until tender, about 30 to 45 minutes. Serve hot. Serves 4.

* If dried mushrooms are used, soak them in a little water a few minutes before cooking.

CHICKEN WITH BRANDY

POLLO CON LIQUORE

1 chicken breast
½ cup butter
1 medium-sized onion, minced
1 jigger brandy
6 tablesp. flour
⅓ cup cream
2 cups chicken or veal stock
Salt and pepper
Pinch of nutmeg
1 tablesp. lemon juice
1 tablesp. marsala or sherry
1 small truffle, sliced thin (optional)

Remove skin from chicken breast and cut into 1 in. pieces. Saute these in 2 tablesp. butter over low flame about 20 minutes. In separate pan fry onion in 2 tablesp. butter until soft. Add onions to sauted chicken, add brandy, and cook over low flame 10 minutes longer. While chicken is cooking, make a white sauce of remaining 4 tablesp. butter, flour, cream, and stock. Season with salt and pepper, and cook over low heat until mixture is thick, stirring constantly. Remove from stove, add remaining ingredients, except truffle, and blend well. Strain through a fine sieve if necessary. Pour this sauce over chicken, garnish with truffle, and serve with cooked rice. Serves 4.

BREAST OF CHICKEN WITH EGG SAUCE

PETTO DI POLLO CON SALSA DI UOVA

2 chicken breasts
Salt and pepper
3 tablesp. butter
2 tablesp. flour
1 cup chicken stock
½ cup light cream
Pinch of nutmeg
1 egg yolk, slightly beaten

Wash chicken breasts, dry, and remove bone. Sprinkle with salt and pepper and saute in butter over medium flame until golden brown on all sides, about 20 minutes. Chicken should be cooked through. Transfer to serving dish and keep hot. Combine flour, chicken stock, and cream, and add to pan in which chicken was fried. Cook over low flame, stirring constantly, until thick and smooth. Add seasonings. Remove from heat, add slightly beaten egg yolk, and return to stove. Cook over very low heat 1 minute longer, stirring constantly, until thick. Strain sauce if it is lumpy, pour over chicken, and serve. Serves 2. Rice or cooked pasta make good accompaniments for this dish.

CHICKEN IN CASSEROLE

POLLO IN CASSARUOLA

1 fryer, 2½ to 3 lbs.
Salt and pepper
2 eggs, slightly beaten
2 tablesp. water
2 cups bread crumbs
6 tablesp. melted butter or oil

Cut chicken into serving pieces, wash, dry, and dust with salt and pepper. Combine slightly beaten eggs and water. Dip pieces of chicken in diluted egg, then roll in crumbs. Let stand in cool place for ½ hour. Grease a casserole or baking dish with butter, and place chicken in casserole. Bake in slow oven 325° until tender, ¾ to 1 hour. Serves 2.

HUNTER'S CHICKEN

POLLO ALLA CACCIATORA

2 broilers, 1½ to 2 lbs.
¼ cup olive oil
2 medium-sized onions, chopped
1 clove garlic, minced
Pinch of oregano (optional)
2 cups canned tomatoes
¼ cup white wine or sherry
1 tablesp. minced parsley
1 cup sliced fresh mushrooms
Salt and pepper

Cut chicken into serving pieces, wash, and dry. Brown chicken in hot oil for about 10 minutes on all sides, over medium flame. Add onion, garlic, oregano, and tomatoes which have been mashed with a fork. Cover pan tightly and simmer 30 minutes. Add wine, parsley, mushrooms, and seasonings. Continue to cook 15 minutes longer, until chicken is tender. Serve hot. Serves 4.

ROMAN CHICKEN CACCIATORA

POLLO CACCIATORA ALLA ROMANA

1 fryer, 1½ to 2 lbs.
½ cup olive or salad oil
1 large onion, minced
1 #2½ can tomatoes
1 lb. button mushrooms
Salt and pepper
½ teasp. oregano (optional)
¾ cup sherry

Have butcher cut chicken into serving pieces. Wash and wipe dry. Brown in ¼ cup hot oil over medium flame, and set aside until needed. Saute onion in remaining oil until soft. Add tomatoes, mash with fork, and simmer 5 minutes, stirring occasionally. Wipe mushrooms with damp cloth, and add to sauce. Add browned chicken and seasonings, cover pan, and simmer until chicken is tender, about 25 minutes. Turn occasionally. Add wine and cook 5 minutes longer. Serve hot with sauce. Serves 3.

FRIED CHICKEN

POLLO FRITTO

2 frying chickens
1 tablesp. salt
2 cups sifted flour
¼ cup grated Parmesan cheese
Salt and pepper
4 eggs, well beaten
2 cups salad oil

Have butcher cut chicken into serving pieces. Marinate chicken in cold water and a pinch of rosemary overnight, if desired. Otherwise, wash chicken and wipe dry. Combine cheese, salt, and pepper, and roll chicken in this mixture. Dip in beaten eggs, and fry in hot oil over high flame until brown. Turn once. Cover pan, reduce heat to low, and cook chicken until tender, about 30 minutes. Drain on unglazed paper. Serve hot or cold. Serves 4.

CHICKEN WITH OLIVES

POLLO CON OLIVE

2 fryers, 2 lbs. each; or, a small duckling, about 4 lbs.
2½ cups water or stock
10 green olives, pitted
2 small onions, sliced
Salt and pepper

Cut bird up into serving pieces, wash, and wipe dry. Chop gizzard, heart, and liver into small pieces. Cook chicken and giblets over medium flame in stock until liquid is reduced to half. Transfer bird to a shallow baking pan or large frying pan. Add stock, olives, and sliced onions. Add seasonings. Cover pan tightly and simmer until tender, about 1 hour. Add a little more liquid, if necessary. Serve hot, garnished with more olives. Serves 6.

CHICKEN WITH RICE

POLLO CON RISO

1 fryer, about 3 lbs.
2 tablesp. butter
3 tablesp. olive oil
⅛ lb. prosciutto, diced; or, ⅛ lb. salt pork
1 medium onion, chopped
1 tablesp. tomato paste
1 teasp. parsley
3 qts. water
Salt and pepper
½ lb. uncooked rice

Cut chicken into serving pieces, wash, and wipe dry. Brown chicken in butter and oil over medium flame. Remove and set aside. Brown ham and onion in same pan about 2 minutes. Transfer ham and onion to a large saucepan, and add tomato paste, parsley, water, and seasonings. Bring this to a boil, then add browned chicken. Cook over low heat 10 minutes. Then add uncooked rice and continue to cook until chicken and rice are done, about 20 minutes. Serve hot, sprinkled with grated cheese. Serves 3.

ROAST STUFFED CHICKEN

POLLO IMBOTTITO

1 roasting chicken, 4 to 6 lbs. *Salt and pepper*

STUFFING:

½ lb. ground beef
2 tablesp. olive oil
1 small onion, chopped
1 celery stalk, chopped
2 ripe tomatoes, peeled and chopped
1 teasp. chopped parsley
1 cup bread crumbs
¼ cup grated Parmesan cheese
Salt and pepper
2 hard-boiled eggs

Wash chicken, wipe dry, and sprinkle with salt and pepper inside and out.

Brown ground meat in oil with onion over medium heat about 10 minutes. Stir occasionally to prevent meat from lumping. Combine meat with remaining ingredients except for hard-boiled eggs, and mix thoroughly. Stuff chicken with half of stuffing. Then insert the whole, peeled, hard-boiled eggs, and then put in the rest of the stuffing. Sew chicken or fasten with skewers. Rub entire chicken with butter, set breast side up in roasting pan, and bake in a moderate oven 350° until chicken is done, about 1½ to 2 hours. Baste occasionally with pan drippings. Serve hot or cold. Serves 4.
CAUTION: If you refrigerate the roasted chicken, be sure to remove all stuffing to a separate bowl.

RICE STUFFING #1

½ cup cooked rice
2 slices Italian salami, chopped
1 onion, chopped
¼ cup grated Parmesan cheese
½ cup bread crumbs
¼ teasp. marjoram
Salt and pepper
2 eggs
2 mushrooms, sliced thin (optional)

Combine all ingredients, and follow directions given above.

RICE STUFFING #2

Substitute 1 link of Italian sweet or hot sausage for salami in Rice Stuffing #1.

RICE STUFFING #3

Substitute 2 slices chopped prosciutto for salami in Rice Stuffing #1.

CHICKEN TETRAZZINI

POLLO TETRAZZINI

1 stewing chicken, 4 to 5 lbs.
Salt and pepper
½ lb. broad noodles, broken into 3 in. pieces
¼ cup butter
1 large onion, chopped
1 green pepper, chopped
¼ lb. fresh mushrooms; or, 1 4-oz. can sliced mushrooms
1½ cups grated Parmesan cheese
¼ cup minced parsley

Cut chicken into serving pieces, wash, and dry. Place chicken, salt, and pepper in enough cold water to cover, bring to a boil, and skim surface. Cover pan and simmer until meat falls from bone, about 2½ to 3 hours.

Strain stock; cut chicken meat into small pieces, and set aside. Bring strained stock to a boil, and boil noodles in soup until tender, about 10 minutes. Drain noodles. While noodles are cooking, saute the onions and chopped pepper in butter, add mushrooms, and saute for 5 minutes until golden brown. Add cheese, chicken, and drained noodles, and heat thoroughly. Serve immediately, sprinkled with parsley. Serves 6.

CHICKEN IN TOMATO SAUCE

POLLO AL SALSA POMODORO

1 roasting chicken, about 4 lbs.
5 tablesp. salad or olive oil
1 recipe Basic Tomato Sauce, see p. 61
½ lb. cooked pasta

Cut chicken into serving pieces, wash, and dry. Saute in oil until brown on all sides. Bring tomato sauce to a boil, add browned chicken, and simmer uncovered till chicken is tender, about 2½ hours. Transfer chicken to serving platter, and pour sauce over pasta. Serve immediately. Serves 6.
NOTE: ½ cup Italian red wine may be added to sauce 15 minutes before chicken is done.

CAPON ROMAN STYLE

CAPPONE ALLA ROMANO

1 capon, 4 to 5 lbs.
¼ lb. salt pork or prosciutto, diced
2 tablesp. olive oil
Salt and pepper
Pinch of sage
1 clove garlic, minced
1½ cups white wine
2 cups canned tomatoes

Have butcher clean capon and cut it into serving pieces. Wash and wipe dry. Sprinkle capon with salt and pepper, and saute with salt pork and oil over medium fire until brown on all sides. Sprinkle with sage and garlic, and add wine and tomatoes. Cover pan and cook over low heat until tender, 2 to 2½ hours. Add a little stock or water if necessary. Serve hot. Serves 5 to 6.

CHICKEN LIVERS WITH MUSHROOMS

FEGATO DI POLLO CON FUNGHI

1 lb. mushrooms
6 tablesp. olive oil or butter
1 medium-sized onion, sliced
1 lb. chicken livers
Salt and pepper
½ cup sauterne or other white wine

Wipe mushrooms with damp cloth, and slice. Saute mushrooms and sliced onion in oil or butter until brown, stirring occasionally. Add chicken livers and cook 5 minutes more. Season with salt and pepper, add wine, and cook 1 minute. Do not allow to boil. Serve hot over toast or rice. Serves 4.

CHICKEN LIVERS WITH TOMATO SAUCE

FEGATO DI POLLO CON SALSA POMODORO

Prepare 1 recipe of Basic Tomato Sauce, see p. 61. After onions have browned, add 1 lb. chopped chicken livers and saute 3 minutes. Then add remaining ingredients, and cook and serve as directed.

VARIATIONS: ½ bay leaf may be added 15 minutes before sauce is done. Or, add ½ lb. fresh shelled peas 20 minutes before sauce is done.

DUCK WITH LENTILS

ANITRA CON LENTICCHI

1 duck, 1½ to 2 lbs.
2 slices salt pork or bacon, chopped
2 tablesp. olive oil
1 medium-sized onion, sliced
1 celery stalk, chopped
1 carrot, chopped
1 tablesp. parsley
1 bay leaf
3 pitted black olives (optional)
Salt and pepper
½ cup brandy or red wine
½ lb. cooked lentils; or, 1 #2 can lentils

Clean and dress duck. Wash inside and out, and wipe dry. Sprinkle inside lightly with salt and pepper. Lay duck in a dutch oven or braising pan, add salt pork or bacon, oil, onion, celery, carrot, and parsley, and brown over medium flame on all sides, about 15 minutes. Turn often so that duck is evenly browned. Add bay leaf, olives, and seasonings. Pour brandy or wine over duck, and cook until liquor evaporates, about 15 minutes. Pour enough boiling water into pan to cover duck, reduce heat, cover pan, and simmer until duck is tender. Do not overcook. Put duck on serving platter. Skim excess fat from pan gravy, and pour gravy over drained lentils. Serve immediately. Serves 2 to 4.

DUCK WITH NOODLES

ANITRA LASAGNE

1 young duckling, 3½ to 4 lbs.
2 tablesp. olive oil or melted butter
½ cup diced onion
1 #2½ can tomatoes
1 large can tomato puree
½ cup red wine
Pinch of oregano
Salt and pepper
1 lb. uncooked lasagne

Have butcher clean duck and cut it into serving pieces. Wash and dry. Set liver aside. Brown duck on all sides in oil or butter over medium heat. Transfer to a large saucepan. Brown onions in same oil, add tomatoes and tomato puree, and simmer 5 minutes. Pour this sauce over duck, add wine, oregano, and seasonings, and cook uncovered over low fire until duck is tender, about 45 minutes. Add chopped duck liver 10 minutes before duck will be done. As sauce cooks, skim the fat from the surface occasionally. While duck is cooking, boil lasagne according to the directions given on p. 37. Drain, and place on serving dish. Take duck out of sauce, and pour sauce over lasagne, mixing thoroughly. Serve duck and lasagne immediately, sprinkled with grated Parmesan cheese, if desired. Serves 6.

STUFFED ROAST DUCK WITH ITALIAN SAUSAGE

ANITRA IMBOTTITA

1 duck, 4 to 5 lbs.
½ lb. Italian bulk sausage
1 cup cooked rice
¼ cup bread crumbs
1 egg
Very little salt and pepper

Have butcher clean duck and cut off tips of wings. Wash inside and out with cold water. Drain dry. Combine sausage, rice, crumbs, egg, and a very little salt and pepper, and stuff duck with mixture. Sew or skewer duck. Place breast up in an uncovered shallow baking pan, and roast uncovered in slow oven 325° until duck is tender, 1½ to 2 hours. Baste occasionally with pan drippings, or with sherry or claret. Serve hot. Serves 4.

DUCK VENETIAN

ANITRA ALLA VENEZIA

1 duck, 1½ to 2 lbs.
Salt and pepper
1 celery stalk, chopped
½ clove garlic, chopped
¼ cup olive oil

Have butcher clean and dress duck. Wash thoroughly and wipe dry. Sprinkle cavity with ½ teasp. salt and ¼ teasp. pepper. Stuff with chopped celery and garlic. Rub outside with oil, and sprinkle outside with 1 teasp. salt. Place duck breast side down in a roasting pan, and roast uncovered in very hot oven 450° until done, about 45 minutes. Baste often with Orange Sauce (see below). Remove stuffing before serving, and serve hot with cooked rice and pan gravy. Serves 2.

ORANGE SAUCE:

2 tablesp. melted butter
½ cup. marsala or red wine
Juice and rind of 1 orange

Combine all ingredients, and warm slightly in a saucepan. Use to baste duck.

DUCK IN WINE

ANITRA IN VINO

1 duck, 5 to 6 lbs.
½ cup Italian vermouth
1 jigger of brandy
Salt and pepper

Have butcher skin duck and cut it into serving pieces. Place pieces in a casserole or baking dish, season with salt and pepper, and pour vermouth and brandy over all. Marinate for 3 hours. Then put duck in a saucepan with marinade, and cook over low flame until duck is tender, about 1 hour. Serve hot. Serves 4.

PARTRIDGE PIEDMONT STYLE

PERNICI ALLA PIEMONTESE

2 young partridges
6 tablesp. drippings from bacon, or salt pork; or, 2 tablesp. lard and 4 tablesp. butter
Salt and pepper
¼ cup water

Select partridges that have yellow feet, which indicates that they are young. Old birds have gray feet. Clean partridges, and wipe with a damp cloth inside and out. Sprinkle inside and out with salt and pepper. Use only a very little salt if you are using bacon or salt pork drippings. Rub the birds with the drippings, and place them in a greased roasting pan. Add ¼ cup water, and bake in a moderate oven 350° until tender, 30 or 40 minutes, depending upon size. Baste occasionally with pan drippings, or, if birds get too dry, with a little water. When birds are done, cut them in half lengthwise. Serve them on a bed of romaine, accompanied with the following Egg Sauce.

EGG SAUCE:

4 egg yolks
1 tablesp. sugar
¼ cup sherry
Pinch of nutmeg

Place egg yolks in top of cold double boiler, and add sugar. Beat until thick and lemon colored. Add wine a little at a

time, beating constantly. Cook over boiling water for five minutes, beating constantly. Boiling water must not touch top of double boiler. *Do not overcook.* Remove from heat, add nutmeg, and serve immediately with partridges. Serves 4.
NOTE: Spring fryers may be prepared in this same way.

BROILED PHEASANT

FAGIANO ALLA GRIGLIA

1 small pheasant, 2 to 2½ lbs.
1 clove garlic, cut in half
3 tablesp. butter
Salt and pepper
¼ cup white wine

Have butcher clean pheasant and split it in half. Wash and wipe dry. Rub pheasant with garlic, and then with butter. Sprinkle inside and out with salt and pepper. Place pheasant on preheated broiling rack skin down, and broil 6 in. from flame for 20 minutes. Turn and broil other side 10 to 15 minutes, until bird is tender and brown. Brush with butter if bird gets too dry. When done, remove from broiler and keep hot. Combine drippings from broiler pan with wine, and heat 1 minute over low flame. *Do not boil.* Pour this sauce over pheasant and serve immediately. Serves 2.
NOTE: 1 domestic guinea hen may be used instead of pheasant.

PANNED QUAIL

QUAGLIA

6 quail
½ cup oil or drippings
1 small onion, chopped
2 cloves garlic
2 anchovy fillets, chopped
1 10-oz. can tomato puree
1 cup white wine
¼ cup pitted green olives, chopped
Salt and pepper

Select white quail. Have butcher clean them. Wash and wipe dry. Brown onion in fat for 1 minute, add garlic, and saute together until brown. Add quail and brown them on all sides over medium fire. Combine cut-up anchovies, tomato puree, and wine, and pour this sauce over birds. Add olives and seasonings. Cover pan and cook over medium flame until tender, about a half hour. Add a little water or stock if birds get too dry. Serve as soon as they are done over buttered toast or boiled rice. Strain sauce and pour it over birds. Serves 6. NOTE: Squab, fryers, or partridges may also be prepared in this way.

STUFFED SQUAB

PICCIONI IMBOTTITI

4 plump squab, ¾ to 1 lb. each
2 cups bread crumbs
3 eggs
¼ cup grated Romano cheese
1 teasp. chopped parsley
1 onion, chopped
Pinch of marjoram
2 tablesp. claret
Salt and pepper
½ cup olive oil or melted lard

Have butcher clean squab. Wash squab, drain dry, and cut off tips of wings. Combine all ingredients except oil and mix well. Stuff cavity of birds with mixture, and sew or skewer closed. Brush each bird with oil and place breast side up in uncovered baking dish. Bake in hot oven 400° until tender and brown, about 30 to 40 minutes. Brush occasionally with oil. If squab get too dry, baste with ¼ cup claret or water. Serve hot. Serves 4.

SQUAB IN TOMATO SAUCE

PICCIONI CON SALSA POMODORO

2 plump squab, quartered
5 tablesp. olive or salad oil
1 recipe Basic Tomato Sauce, see p. 61

Prepare 1 recipe Basic Tomato Sauce, and simmer uncovered 1½ hours. Brown squab in oil over medium flame. Then add to tomato sauce and cook 1 hour longer, until sauce is thick. Serve with pasta. Serves 4.

STUFFED HOLIDAY TURKEY

TACCHINO DI FESTA

8 to 10 lb. turkey

Have butcher clean bird. Wipe with a damp cloth and cut off oil sac at base of tail. Cut tips off wings. Stuff with one of the following stuffings, and roast in a moderate oven 350° until tender, about 3 hours. Baste occasionally with pan drippings, or, if turkey gets too dry, with olive oil.

STUFFINGS FOR HOLIDAY TURKEY

I.

Slice of salami, ⅛ in. thick
4 scallions; or, 1 small onion
1 truffle; or, 3 large mushrooms
20 chestnuts, blanched and shelled
½ lb. Italian fresh sweet sausage
½ lb. ground veal
½ cup grated Parmesan cheese
Pinch of nutmeg
1 egg
2 tablesp. sauterne, sherry, or other white wine
1 teasp. honey
Salt and pepper
3 tablesp. olive oil

Put salami, onion, mushrooms and chestnuts through food chopper, using medium blade. Remove sausage from casing. Add sausage, and remaining ingredients to chopped mixture and blend well. Stuff body cavity and neck of turkey, and sew or skewer closed. Roast as directed.

II.

Heart, liver, and gizzard of turkey, cooked and chopped
½ lb. Italian sweet sausage, skinned
½ lb. ground veal
3 slices prosciutto, minced
12 chestnuts, pureed
2 eggs, slightly beaten
4 mushrooms, sliced
2 cooked prunes, pitted and chopped
Pinch of nutmeg
⅓ cup grated Parmesan or Romano cheese
1 teasp. honey
White wine to moisten
3 tablesp. olive oil
Salt and pepper

Combine all ingredients and mix thoroughly. Stuff body cavity and neck of turkey, and sew or skewer closed. Roast as directed.

CHAPTER NINE

Egg Dishes

BRAINS WITH EGGS: *See p. 77.*

CAPOCOLLO WITH EGGS

UOVA CON CAPOCOLLO

2 tablesp. olive oil
2 slices capocollo, 1/8 in. thick
2 eggs
Salt and pepper

Pour oil in frying pan, and arrange slices of capocollo in oil. Break 1 egg over each slice of meat, sprinkle very lightly with salt and pepper, and fry gently until egg white is set. Remove with pancake turner, and serve immediately. Serves 1.

CHEESE OMELET

FRITTATA DI FORMAGGIO

6 eggs
1/4 cup olive oil
1/4 lb. mozzarella or provolone cheese, diced

Beat eggs slightly with fork, just enough to blend whites and yolks. Brown cheese in hot oil over medium flame, stirring constantly. Pour beaten eggs over browned cheese, reduce flame to low, and cook gently until the bottom of the omelet is light brown. Turn omelet; hold a flat round plate over top of frying pan, and turn pan over, so that omelet comes out on plate. Then pour omelet oil back in pan, and slide omelet back. Brown other side of omelet, adding more oil if necessary, and serve at once. Serves 6.

EGG SALAD: *See p. 170.*

EGGS WITH MUSHROOMS

UOVA CON FUNGHI

12 mushrooms, sliced
3 tablesp. olive oil
2 tablesp. sherry
6 eggs, slightly beaten

Saute mushrooms in oil over medium flame until brown, stirring occasionally. Season with salt and pepper, reduce heat, add wine, and simmer 3 minutes. Pour eggs in pan over mushrooms, and stir gently until eggs set. Serve hot over buttered toast. Serves 3.

FRIED BREAD AND EGGS

PANE FRITTATA

½ cup salad or olive oil
6 eggs, slightly beaten
3 tablesp. grated Parmesan cheese
Pinch of marjoram
Salt and pepper
6 slices Italian bread
1 cup milk

Combine slightly beaten eggs, cheese, marjoram, and seasonings. Heat oil in frying pan. Dip bread 1 slice at a time into milk, but do not soak. Then dip in seasoned eggs, and saute in hot oil until golden brown. Serve immediately. Serves 3. Excellent as a Lenten side dish.

OMELET PEASANT STYLE

FRITTATA ALLA PAESANA

¼ lb. Italian hot or sweet sausage
2 tablesp. olive oil
6 eggs

Cut sausage into 1 in. pieces and brown in oil over medium heat for 10 minutes, stirring frequently. Beat eggs until light and fluffy. Reduce heat, and pour beaten eggs on sausage, and cook until eggs are thick and creamy. Serve very hot. Serves 4.

OMELET TURIN STYLE

FRITTATA TORINO

¾ lb. diced mozzarella cheese
1 cup milk
6 egg yolks; or, 3 eggs
3 tablesp. butter
Pepper

Combine cheese and milk, and let stand overnight. Drain and reserve 6 tablesp. milk. Beat eggs until light and fluffy. Melt butter in saucepan, and when it is sizzling, add cheese and 6 tablesp. milk. Cook slowly over very low flame until cheese is completely melted, stirring constantly. Remove from heat, add beaten eggs and pepper, and return to stove. Cook slowly, stirring constantly until mixture is thick and cheese is a little hard, about 5 minutes. Taste, and season with salt, if necessary. Serve immediately over toast or cooked rice. Serves 4.

POACHED EGGS

UOVA AFFOGATE

2 tablesp. butter
⅓ cup madeira or sherry
4 eggs
2 tablesp. grated Parmesan cheese
Salt and pepper
4 slices of toast

Melt butter in a shallow casserole or skillet, add wine, and bring it to a boil. Remove from stove. Break eggs 1 at a time into warm wine, sprinkle with cheese, salt, and pepper, and bake in a moderate oven 350° until eggs are firm. Remove from oven, lift eggs out of casserole, and put on slices of hot toast. Serve at once. Serves 2. If desired, you may garnish the eggs with 1 sliced truffle.

POACHED EGGS WITH PEAS

UOVA CON PISELLI

¼ cup olive oil
1 small onion, chopped
2 large potatoes, cubed
1 qt. water
Salt and pepper
2 lbs. fresh peas, shelled
2 tablesp. minced parsley
6 eggs

Saute onion in oil until soft. Add potatoes to pan, and cook 10 minutes over medium flame, stirring occasionally to prevent sticking. Add water and seasonings, and bring to a boil. Add shelled peas and parsley, cover pan, and cook over medium heat until potatoes are tender. Reduce flame, and break eggs into pan. Do not stir. Cook slowly until egg whites are firm; when they are done, serve immediately, using a large spoon to transfer to serving dish. Serves 4.

SCRAMBLED EGGS WITH ONION

UOVA CON CIPOLLA

4 medium-sized onions, sliced
½ cup olive oil
6 eggs
Salt and pepper

Fry onions in oil until golden brown, about 5 minutes. While onions are cooking, beat eggs, salt, and pepper until well blended. Pour beaten eggs over browned onion, and reduce heat to low. Cook 3 minutes, until eggs are moist but not runny, stirring constantly with a fork. Serve hot. May be used as an entree or as a sandwich filling. Serves 3.

SCRAMBLED EGGS WITH TOMATOES

UOVA CON POMODORO

1 #2 can Italian plum tomatoes
Salt and pepper
6 eggs

Pour canned tomatoes into a skillet and simmer over medium flame 10 minutes. Mash occasionally with a fork. While tomatoes are cooking, beat eggs with salt and pepper until well blended. Pour eggs over cooked tomatoes and reduce heat to low. Cook until most of the juice has evaporated, about 5 minutes. Serve hot as an entree or side dish. Serves 4. VARIATION: 1 #2 can of peas may be substituted for tomatoes. Proceed as directed, but do not mash peas.

SCRAMBLED EGGS WITH VERMICELLI

FRITTATA DI UOVA CON VERMICELLI

½ lb. vermicelli, broken into 1 in. pieces
1 tablesp. butter
5 eggs
3 tablesp. grated Parmesan cheese
¼ cup minced parsley
Salt and pepper

Cook vermicelli in 2 qts. salted water 15 minutes. Add butter to water, and stir. Combine eggs, cheese, parsley, and pepper, and mix just enough to blend whites and yolks. Pour beaten eggs into vermicelli and stir slowly over low heat for

2 minutes, until eggs are thick and creamy. Serve immediately. Serves 4.

TRIPE BOLOGNA: *See p. 82.*

SICILIAN EGGS WITH ANCHOVIES

UOVA CON ACCIUGHE

¼ cup olive oil
3 anchovy fillets
1 small onion, sliced
1 cup diced celery
2 sweet green peppers, diced
1 6-oz. can tomato paste
3 cups water
8 hard-boiled eggs, sliced
Salt and pepper

Cook oil, anchovies, onion, celery, and peppers slowly 10 minutes. Stir occasionally to prevent sticking. Blend tomato paste and water and add. Season with a very little salt and pepper. Cover pan and simmer until celery is tender, stirring occasionally.

Put ¼ cup sauce on the bottom of a serving dish. Over this place a layer of hard-boiled egg slices. Alternate layers of sauce and eggs, finishing with sauce. Serve hot or cold. Serves 6.

VEGETABLE OMELET

FRITTATA DI UOVA VERDURA

1 lb. fresh dandelion greens
6 tablesp. olive oil
6 eggs
2 tablesp. grated Romano or Parmesan cheese
Salt and pepper

Remove wilted leaves from dandelion greens, cut off roots, and wash thoroughly under cold water. Do not drain, since the water that will cling to the leaves will serve as cooking liquid. Cut greens into 2 in. pieces, and saute in oil over medium flame until tender, stirring once.

Combine eggs, cheese and seasonings, and beat only enough to blend yolks and white. Pour beaten eggs over cooked dandelions, reduce heat to low, and cook until under side of omelet is brown. Turn omelet and brown other side. Serve hot or cold as a main dish, side dish or sandwich filling. Serves 6.

CHAPTER TEN

Vegetables

STUFFED ARTICHOKES SICILIAN STYLE

CARCIOFI IMBOTTITI ALLA SICILIANA

4 medium-sized artichokes
1 cup bread crumbs
1 clove garlic, chopped
2 anchovy fillets, chopped
1 teasp. chopped parsley
3 tablesp. grated Romano cheese
Salt and pepper
¼ cup olive oil
1 cup cold water

Select compact, heavy artichokes with dark leaves. Wash, and remove large outer leaves around base. Cut off stems, and with a scissors trim point 1½ in. down from top. Spread leaves apart gently. Combine crumbs, garlic, anchovies, parsley, cheese, salt, pepper, and oil, and mix thoroughly. Place crumb mixture between loosened artichoke leaves. Stand artichokes straight up in saucepan, and pour water into pan from side. Do not pour water over artichokes. Cover pan and simmer until leaves pull off easily, about half-hour. Lift out of pan gently. Serve hot or cold. Serves 4.

ASPARAGUS BUNDLES FLORENTINE

SPARAGIO ALLA FIORENTINA

bunch fresh asparagus, about 2 lbs.
6 to 8 thin slices prosciutto
¼ cup butter
¼ cup grated cheese

Select young tender asparagus. Snap off tough stem ends, and wash each stalk well until all sand has been removed. Cook asparagus in salted water 10 minutes over medium flame. Drain. Roll 1 strip prosciutto around 5 asparagus stalks and fasten with toothpick. Grease the bottom of a baking dish with butter and lay bundles in pan. Sprinkle with cheese, and bake in hot oven 400° 5 minutes, until cheese is melted; or, broil 3 to 5 minutes. Serve immediately. Serves 4.
NOTE: Canned asparagus may be used instead of fresh. Drain, wrap with prosciutto, and bake as directed.

BROCCOLI WITH PROSCIUTTO

BROCCOLI CON PROSCIUTTO

1 small bunch of broccoli, about 1½ lbs.
1 clove garlic, chopped fine
3 tablesp. olive oil
⅛ lb. sliced prosciutto
3 tablesp. grated Parmesan cheese
Salt and pepper

Parboil broccoli 10 minutes in a small amount of salted water. Drain. Saute garlic in oil until light brown. Add broccoli and season with pepper. Cook slowly over low flame 5 minutes, adding a little of the water in which broccoli was cooked if pan gets too dry. Add prosciutto and cook 2 minutes longer. Serve immediately, sprinkled with grated cheese. Serves 4 or 5.
VARIATION: Substitute ⅛ lb. pitted black Italian olives for the prosciutto, and prepare as directed.

BROCCOLI MILANESE

BROCCOLI ALLA MILANESE

1 bunch broccoli
¼ cup melted butter
1 cup grated Parmesan cheese
4 poached or fried eggs
Pepper

Boil broccoli in small amount of salted water until almost tender. Drain well and put in baking dish. Pour melted butter over broccoli, sprinkle with cheese and pepper, and bake in moderate oven 375° until cheese is melted, about 5 minutes. Poach or fry eggs while broccoli is baking. Serve broccoli as soon as cheese melts, and put an egg over each portion. Serves 4.
VARIATION: Asparagus stalks may be used in place of broccoli.

BROCCOLI PARMESAN

BROCCOLI ALLA PARMIGIANA

1 large bunch of broccoli
Salt and pepper
¼ cup olive oil or melted butter
¼ cup grated Parmesan cheese

Put broccoli in small amount of water, season with salt and pepper, add oil, and cover pan tightly. Steam until tender, and drain. Put in a hot serving dish, pour pan juices over broccoli, and sprinkle with grated Parmesan cheese. Serve immediately. Serves 4 to 6.

BURDOCK PATTIES

BARDANA FRITTA

1 lb. fresh burdock
Salt and pepper
1 cup flour
½ cup olive oil

Remove outer leaves and wash burdock under cold running water until thoroughly clean. Cut stalks into 2 in. pieces. Cook in 1 qt. boiling salted water in covered pan until tender, 10 to 15 minutes. Drain and let stand for 5 minutes. Sprinkle with

pepper. Shape into patties about 2½ in. in diameter, and ½ in. thick. Dip patties in flour until well coated, and fry in hot oil until golden brown on all sides. Serve hot. Serves 4.
VARIATION: Add 1 cup bread crumbs and ¼ cup grated Parmesan cheese to the cooked burdock, shape into patties, and fry. Omit use of flour.

CABBAGE BUNDLES

CAVOLO PACCO

1 large head of cabbage, 2-3 lbs.
½ lb. ground beef, lamb, or veal
1 cup cooked spinach
½ cup grated Parmesan cheese
2 tablesp. chopped parsley
2 eggs, slightly beaten
¼ teasp. nutmeg (optional)
Salt and pepper
¼ cup olive oil

Discard any wilted cabbage leaves. Remove 12 or 14 large outside leaves. (An easy way to do this is to cut core of cabbage out with a sharp knife, thus freeing core end of leaves. Leaves will then peel off from the bottom.) Drop leaves into boiling salted water, and simmer until limp, but not soft, about 2-3 minutes. Remove from water with slotted spoon, and drain in a colander.

Combine ground meat, spinach, cheese, parsley, eggs, nutmeg, salt, and pepper. Mix thoroughly. Place 2 heaping tablesp. of meat in center of each cabbage leaf. Fold the leaves around the filling, and tie them closed with soft white twine, to prevent the stuffing from falling out. Or, lay the bundles flat so that the open end of the leaf is down.

Place bundles in a shallow baking pan side by side. Pour olive oil over them, and bake in a moderate oven 325° until cabbage is tender, about 25-30 minutes. If pan becomes dry, add ⅔ cup water or stock. Serve hot. Serves 6.

VARIATION: Substitute the following stuffing:

½ lb. ground beef; or
¼ lb. ground veal and
¼ lb. ground pork
6 tablesp. grated Parmesan cheese
½ cup bread crumbs
1 teasp. minced parsley
½ clove garlic, chopped; or, 1 scallion, chopped
Salt and pepper

Combine all ingredients, and mix well. Cook as directed above.

BAKED CAULIFLOWER

CAVOLFIORE AL FORNO

1 medium-sized head cauliflower
1 tablesp. olive oil
¼ cup bread crumbs
¼ cup grated Parmesan cheese
¼ cup olive oil

Remove outer leaves, core, and stalk of cauliflower. Wash and break into flowerets. Cook cauliflower in small amount of boiling salted water until half done, about 6 minutes. Drain. Grease bottom of baking pan with 1 tablesp. olive oil, and arrange cauliflower on the bottom of the pan. Combine crumbs and cheese and sprinkle over cauliflower. Season with pepper. Drizzle ¼ cup olive oil on top of cauliflower, and bake in a moderate oven 350° 30 minutes. If pan becomes too dry, add ¼ cup water. Serve hot. Serves 4.

CAULIFLOWER FRITTERS

CAVOLFIORE FRITTELE

Wash and remove outer leaves of 1 small head of cauliflower. Leave whole, and cook for 15 minutes in a small amount of boiling salted water. Drain and cool. While cauliflower is cooling, prepare batter:

1 cup sifted flour
1 teasp. baking powder
1 teasp. salt
Pepper
1 egg, well beaten
2 tablesp. grated Parmesan cheese
1 cup milk
1 tablesp. salad oil

Sift flour, baking powder, salt, and pepper together in a mixing bowl. Blend egg, cheese, and milk well, and add gradually to dry ingredients. Stir until smooth. *Do not beat.*

Pour 2 cups of oil into a deep frying pan and heat to 375°. Break cauliflower into flowerets and dip into batter. Then fry in oil until golden brown, 2 to 5 minutes. Do not fry more than 3 at one time. Lift fritters from oil and drain on unglazed paper. Serve hot or cold. Serves 4.

CAULIFLOWER SICILIAN STYLE

CAVOLFIORE ALLA SICILIANA

1 small head cauliflower
2 cups water
1 teasp. salt
5 tablesp. olive oil
1 clove garlic
5 anchovy fillets, chopped
Pepper

Separate cauliflower into flowerets, and cook in 2 cups boiling salted water over medium flame until tender, about 10 minutes. Drain and reserve ¼ cup liquid. Brown garlic in oil for 3 minutes, and then remove it from pan. Add anchovies to same oil, and stir until anchovies are reduced to a paste. Add reserved cauliflower liquid, and cook 5 minutes. Put cooked cauliflower in hot serving dish, sprinkle with pepper, and pour anchovy sauce over it. Toss lightly, and serve at once. Serves 4 to 6. This is also good cold.

SMOTHERED DANDELION GREENS

CICORIA AFFOGATA

2 lbs. fresh dandelion greens
3 tablesp. olive oil
1 clove garlic, chopped
Salt and pepper

Discard wilted dandelion leaves. Wash greens several times in cold water and cut off roots. Saute garlic in hot oil for 1 minute. Add washed greens and seasonings. Cover pan tightly and cook slowly 10 to 12 minutes until tender. If pan becomes too dry, add 2 tablesp. water. Stir occasionally. Serve hot as vegetable with meat, fish, or poultry. Serves 4.

DANDELION GREENS OMELET: *See* Vegetable Omelet, *p. 138.*

BREADED EGGPLANT

MELENZANA IMPANATA

1 medium-sized eggplant
1 tablesp. salt
2 eggs, well beaten
1 cup bread crumbs
¼ cup grated Romano or Parmesan cheese
Pinch of pepper
1 teasp. minced basil
2 cups salad or peanut oil

Wash eggplant, but do not pare. Slice lengthwise into ¼ in. slices. Sprinkle salt on each side of eggplant slices and place them in a colander. Cover slices with a plate so that it presses down on them, and put a weight on it. Let slices stand for 1 hour, then squeeze dry with hands.

Dip each slice in beaten eggs, then roll in crumbs combined with cheese, pepper, and basil. Heat oil in frying pan, and saute eggplant until golden brown and soft over medium flame. Drain on unglazed paper and serve hot. Serves 3 to 4.

FRIED EGGPLANT

MELENZANA FRITTA

1 large eggplant
1 tablesp. salt
1 cup olive oil
Pepper
½ cup grated Romano cheese

Wash eggplant, but do not pare. Slice in ¼ in. slices, sprinkle salt on each slice, and let stand 1 hour in colander. Squeeze dry with palms of hands. Heat oil in frying pan and fry eggplant until brown on each side over medium flame. Sprinkle with pepper and grated cheese, and serve hot or cold. May be used as antipasto, side dish, entree, or sandwich filling. Serves 4.

EGGPLANT AND LASAGNE SICILIAN STYLE

MELENZANA E LASAGNE ALLA SICILIANA

1 medium-sized eggplant
2 tablesp. olive oil
1 clove garlic, chopped
1 6-oz. can tomato paste
3 cups water
½ cup grated Parmesan cheese
½ lb. cooked lasagne
Salt and pepper

Wash eggplant, but do not pare. Slice it ¼ in. thick, sprinkle slices with salt, and let stand in a colander 30 minutes. While eggplant is standing, prepare sauce. Fry the chopped garlic in 2 tablesp. olive oil until brown, then add tomato paste and water, blending well. Simmer uncovered 30 minutes.

While sauce is cooking, finish preparing eggplant. Squeeze each slice dry, and fry in ½ cup oil until golden brown on all sides. Remove from pan and drain on absorbent paper.

When sauce is done, put a layer of eggplant and a layer of cooked lasagne in an ungreased baking dish. Pour sauce over them, sprinkle with cheese, and add salt and pepper if necessary. Repeat until ingredients are all used, ending with a layer of sauce. Bake in moderate oven 375° until firm. Do not overcook. Serve hot. Serves 6.

EGGPLANT WITH PICKLED VEGETABLES

CAPALATINA

2 large eggplant
1 tablesp. salt
¾ cup olive oil
2 onions, chopped
1 #2 can Italian plum tomatoes
¼ lb. Italian green olives, pitted
3 celery stalks, diced
¼ cup capers
¼ cup wine vinegar
2 tablesp. sugar
Salt and pepper

Wash eggplant, but do not pare. Cut into 1 in. cubes, sprinkle with salt, and let stand in a colander 2 hours. Squeeze dry with palms of hands. Heat oil in saucepan, and saute eggplant over medium flame until soft. Turn constantly so that eggplant will be brown on all sides. Remove from pan with slotted spoon and drain off as much oil as possible. Use oil to brown chopped onions until soft, then add strained tomatoes, olives, and celery. Cook slowly until celery is tender, about 15 minutes. Return eggplant to pan, and add capers. Heat vinegar, dissolve sugar in it, and pour this mixture over eggplant. Taste and correct seasoning with salt and pepper. Cover pan and cook slowly over medium flame for 20 minutes, stirring occasionally to prevent sticking. Serve hot or cold as antipasto or vegetable. Keeps well in refrigerator. Serves 6.

EGGPLANT IN VINEGAR

MELENZANA CON ACETO

1 large eggplant, about 2 lbs.
1 clove garlic, minced
½ cup wine vinegar
1 teasp. oregano
Salt and pepper
1 cup olive oil

Wash eggplant, but do not pare. Cut into 1½ in. cubes. Cook in boiling water over medium flame 10 minutes, *no longer*. Eggplant must not get mushy. Drain cubes well. Combine remaining ingredients, and blend well. Pour dressing over eggplant cubes and toss lightly with fingers until well mixed. Place in quart jar, cover, and keep in refrigerator until ready to use. Serve as a side dish with meat, fowl, and fish, or as an antipasto. Will keep indefinitely. Serves 6.

BOILED FAVAS

FAVA BOLLITO

1 lb. dry fava beans
Salt and pepper
3 tablesp. olive oil

Soak beans overnight. Drain, cover with salted water, and cook over low flame until shells are loose, 2 to 3 hours. Add more water if necessary. Drain, season with salt and pepper, add oil, and serve hot or cold.

STUFFED ESCAROLE LEAVES

ESCAROLA IMBOTTITA

2 heads escarole
½ lb. ground beef or Italian sweet sausage
6 tablesp. olive oil
4 anchovy fillets, chopped
1 clove garlic, chopped
1½ tablesp. minced parsley
4 green olives, pitted and chopped
4 black olives, pitted and chopped
½ cup bread crumbs
1 tablesp. pine nuts (optional)
Salt and pepper
3 tablesp. stock or water

Discard wilted escarole leaves, and wash heads under cold running water. Soak heads while other ingredients are being prepared.

Brown meat in oil over medium flame for 10 minutes, stirring occasionally. If sausage is being used, reduce oil to 2 tablesp. Remove meat from stove, add anchovies, garlic, parsley, olives, crumbs, pine nuts, and a very little salt and pepper, and mix thoroughly. Divide mixture into 2 parts.

Drain escarole. Push leaves apart from center, so that head will lie flat. Place meat mixture in center of head, then close leaves lightly with hands and press together. Place stuffed escarole heads in a frying pan close together. Sprinkle with balance of oil, add soup stock, cover tightly, and cook over medium flame until tender, 18 to 20 minutes. Watch carefully, and add a little more liquid if necessary. Remove carefully from pan with pancake turner, and serve immediately. Serves 6.

NOTE: White string may be used to tie leaves closed, if desired.

FENNEL FLORENTINE

FINOCCHIO ALLA FIORENTINO

6 small stalks of fennel
2 tablesp. olive oil or melted butter
1 clove garlic
¼ cup water
Salt and pepper
¼ cup grated Parmesan cheese

Discard coarse outer stalks and ends of fennel. Cut into 1 in. pieces, and wash well. Combine fennel, oil, garlic, water, and seasonings in a large pan. Cover tightly and steam until tender, about 30 minutes. Add more water if necessary. Serve hot, sprinkled with cheese, as a side dish with meat, fish, fowl, or game. Serves 6.

SAUTEED FENNEL

FINOCCHIO SAUTE

1 ½ lbs. fennel
6 cups water
Salt
1 clove garlic
2 tablesp. olive oil

Select fennel with white hearts and dark green leaves. Wash thoroughly under cold water, remove tough outer leaves, cut tender leaves in half, and cut hearts into quarters. Bring salted water to a boil, add fennel, cover, and cook slowly until tender, about 10 minutes. Drain. Saute garlic in hot oil until brown, remove garlic from pan, and add fennel. Saute for 3 minutes, dust with pepper, and serve immediately. Serves 4.

KOHLRABI IN SKILLET

CAVOLRAPA FRITTE

1 bunch fresh kohlrabi, 5 small knobs
¼ cup olive oil
1 clove garlic
1 #2 can tomatoes
Salt and pepper
Pinch of marjoram

Discard wilted leaves. Wash kohlrabi, peel, and cut knobs in 1 in. pieces. Remove leaves from stalks, and chop smaller leaves. Saute garlic in oil 2 minutes. Remove garlic, and add tomatoes. Cook over low flame for 5 minutes, then add kohlrabi and chopped leaves. Season with salt, pepper, and marjoram, cover tightly, and simmer until tender, 20 to 30 minutes. Stir occasionally. Serve hot as a side dish with meat, fish, and fowl. Serves 4.

MUSHROOMS IN WINE

FUNGHI CON VINO

¾ lb. fresh button mushrooms
¼ cup olive oil
1 large onion, sliced thin
Salt and pepper
½ cup sherry, marsala, or white wine

Wipe mushrooms with a damp cloth. Saute whole in oil over medium flame 5 minutes. Add onions and cook 7 minutes more, stirring occasionally. Add seasonings and wine, and heat an additional 3 minutes. *Do not allow to boil.* Serve hot with steak, as a main dish over buttered toast or rice, or as a vegetable. Serves 4 to 6.

SAUTEED MUSHROOMS

FUNGHI ALLA FRITTE

1 lb. fresh small mushrooms
1 clove garlic, chopped; or 1 small onion, sliced
3 tablesp. olive oil
Salt and pepper

Wipe mushrooms with a damp cloth. Saute whole in oil with garlic and seasonings over low flame until tender, about 10 minutes. Serve hot with meat or fowl. Serves 4.

STUFFED MUSHROOMS

FUNGHI RIPIENE

1 lb. fresh mushrooms
½ cup bread crumbs
¼ cup grated Parmesan or Romano cheese
Salt and pepper
Pinch of oregano (optional)
¼ cup olive oil

Wipe mushrooms with a damp cloth, and remove stems. Place in a shallow baking pan. Combine crumbs, cheese, seasonings, and oregano, and sprinkle this mixture over mushrooms. Dribble oil over all, and bake in a moderate oven 350° until tender, about 15 minutes. If mushrooms become too dry, add 1 tablesp. water. Do not overcook. Serve immediately. Serves 4.

BOILED MUSTARD GREENS

BOLLITO MOSTARDA

2 lbs. fresh mustard greens
¼ cup olive or salad oil
½ clove garlic

Remove wilted leaves and roots, and wash greens under cold running water. Drain. Cook in covered pan in boiling salted water until tender, about 10 minutes. Brown garlic in oil about 3 minutes, add to greens, and cook 1 minute longer. Season with pepper, and serve immediately. Serves 6.

PEAS WITH HAM

PISELLI CON PROSCIUTTO

2 lbs. fresh peas, shelled and washed; or, 1 pkg. frozen peas
¼ cup oil or melted butter
3 tablesp. water or soup stock
Salt and pepper
¼ lb. prosciutto, chopped

Heat oil in saucepan, add peas, water, and seasonings. Cover pan, and simmer 15 minutes, stirring occasionally. If water becomes absorbed, add a little more. Add chopped ham, and continue to cook until peas are tender. Serve hot. Serves 4.
VARIATION: Substitute 1 lb. fresh string beans, or 1 pkg.

frozen string beans for peas. When using frozen vegetables, cut down on cooking time.

PEAS PARMESAN

PISELLI ALLA PARMIGIANA

2 lbs. fresh shelled peas; or, 1 pkg. frozen peas, unthawed
¼ cup olive oil
6 scallions, minced
¼ cup fresh mint, parsley, or chopped basil
Salt and pepper
Grated Parmesan cheese

Saute onion in hot oil until light brown. Add ¼ cup water, peas, mint, and seasonings. Cover tightly and steam until peas are tender, 7 or 8 minutes for young peas, 15 for large peas. Serve hot, sprinkled with cheese. Serves 4.

STUFFED GREEN PEPPERS AGRIGENTO

PEPERONI IMBOTTITI ALLA AGRIGENTO

4 large green peppers
¼ cup olive oil
1 small onion, chopped; or, 1 clove garlic, chopped
½ lb. ground veal, pork, or beef
¼ cup grated Parmesan cheese
1½ cups cooked rice
1 tablesp. chopped parsley
Salt and pepper
2 tablesp. red wine (optional)
Strained juice from 1 #2 can Italian tomatoes

Wash peppers. Cut a thin slice from stem end, and remove seeds and pith. Do not cut into two pieces. Brown onion or garlic and ground meat in oil over medium flame until meat is no longer red. Stir occasionally. Remove pan from heat, and add remaining ingredients except tomato juice. Mix thoroughly. Stuff hollow of peppers with meat. Grease bottom of baking sheet with olive oil, and stand the stuffed peppers upright in pan. Pour strained tomato juice around peppers and bake in moderate oven 350° until tender, 30 minutes. Baste occasionally with pan liquid, and if pan gets too dry, add a little stock or water. Serve hot. Serves 4.

POLENTA WITH SAUSAGE

POLENTA CON SALSICCIA

1 lb. sweet or hot Italian sausage
1 small onion
1 tablesp. olive oil
1 #2 can tomatoes
Salt and pepper
1 cup yellow corn meal
1 cup grated Parmesan cheese

Brown sausage and onion in oil over medium flame. Add tomatoes, and seasonings. Simmer for 1 hour, stirring occasionally. While sauce is cooking, prepare corn meal. Bring 1½ qts. salted water to a boil, and pour corn meal into water, stirring constantly to prevent lumping. Cook uncovered over low heat until corn meal leaves sides of pan, about 30 minutes. Watch carefully and stir constantly. Remove from flame and stir in ½ cup grated cheese. Pour half the corn meal on a large platter. Pour ½ the sauce over corn meal, and sprinkle with half of remaining cheese. Repeat layers and serve at once. Serves 4.

POTATO PATTIES

ARANCINI DI PATATE

3 medium-sized potatoes
½ cup bread crumbs
¼ cup grated Parmesan cheese
2 teasp. chopped parsley (optional)
1 egg, slightly beaten
2 tablesp. sherry
Salt and pepper
1 egg, well beaten
1 cup bread crumbs
½ cup olive oil

Peel and quarter potatoes, and boil in salted water until tender. Press through a ricer, or mash very fine. Add crumbs, cheese, parsley, slightly beaten egg, wine, and seasonings. Mix thoroughly and form into patties 2½ in. in diameter and ½ in. thick. Dip patties in well beaten egg, then in bread crumbs. Fry in hot oil until golden brown on both sides, about 3 minutes. Serve hot. Serves 3.

RICE BALLS

ARANCINI DI RISO

½ lb. uncooked rice
3 tablesp. olive oil
1 lb. ground steak
Salt and pepper
¼ cup grated Parmesan cheese
2 eggs, well beaten
1 cup bread crumbs
2 cups salad or peanut oil

Cook rice in 2 qts. boiling water until kernels crush easily between thumb and finger. Drain and cool slightly.

While rice is cooking, brown meat in oil over medium flame. Season with salt and pepper, add grated cheese, and blend well. Cool. Place 2 tablesp. cooked rice in the palm of the hand. Make a well in rice and put in 1 heaping tablesp. of meat mixture. Mold rice around meat into a ball. Dip balls in beaten eggs and roll in crumbs. Fry in deep hot oil until golden brown on both sides, about 3 minutes. Do not fry more than 3 at a time. Remove balls from oil with a slotted spoon and serve immediately. Arancini may be served either as a vegetable, or as a main dish. Serves 6.

RICE WITH CHOPPED MEAT SAUCE

RISO CON SALSA DI CARNE

1 recipe Chopped Meat Sauce, see p. 55
1 lb. uncooked rice
Salt and pepper
½ cup grated Parmesan or Romano cheese

Prepare sauce first, following directions given on p. 55. When it is nearly done, prepare rice by boiling it without stirring over a low fire in 4 qts. water for 15 minutes. Drain. Combine cooked rice, half of meat sauce, and half of cheese, and mix until rice is well coated. Serve hot, topped with additional meat sauce and cheese. Serves 6. This dish is a favorite one for St. Lucy's Day, since it is a Sicilian custom not to eat any food made with flour on that day.

RICE PIEDMONT STYLE

RISO PIEMONTESE

¼ cup butter
1 small onion, minced
¼ lb. prosciutto, slivered; or, ¼ cup chopped chicken giblets
¼ cup mushrooms
2 cups uncooked rice
2 qts. stock

Saute onion in butter over medium flame until light brown. Add prosciutto and heat thoroughly. Add mushrooms and uncooked rice. Stir over low flame until butter is absorbed, about 5 minutes. Add 3 cups stock, and cook over low flame, stirring constantly, until rice is tender. Add more stock whenever necessary. Rice should be moist, but not soupy. Serve hot, sprinkled with grated cheese. Serves 6 to 8.

RICE PUFFS

RISO SFINGE

¼ cup uncooked rice
2 cups milk
1 teasp. butter
3 eggs, separated
1 jigger of rum
⅓ cup flour
2 cups peanut or salad oil

Cook rice in milk over a low flame until kernels are tender, about 20 minutes. Season with salt, and pour into a dish. Do not drain. Add butter and mix well. Add slightly beaten egg yolks, rum, and flour, and blend thoroughly. Beat egg whites until stiff but not dry, and fold them into rice mixture.

Heat oil to 370°. Make puffs by dropping 1 heaping teasp. of rice mixture into hot oil. Do not fry more than 3 puffs at one time, or temperature of oil will drop. Fry puffs until golden brown on both sides. Remove from oil with slotted spoon, sprinkle with powdered sugar and serve immediately. These puffs may be used either as a vegetable side dish, or as a dessert. Enough for 3.

RICE TUSCAN STYLE

RISO ALLA TOSCANO

3 tablesp. butter
½ onion, sliced
2 chicken livers, chopped
2 sweetbreads, chopped
1 thin slice prosciutto, slivered
2 mushrooms, chopped
1 truffle, sliced thin (optional)
¼ cup sherry
⅝ cup uncooked rice
2 cups stock or water
Pinch of nutmeg
Salt and pepper
2 tablesp. grated Parmesan cheese

Saute onion, livers, sweetbreads, prosciutto, and mushrooms in butter until brown, stirring frequently. Add truffles and wine. Add washed, uncooked rice, and simmer over low flame until wine has evaporated. Add stock and seasonings, and cook until rice is tender, about 20 minutes. Serve immediately, sprinkled with grated Parmesan cheese. Serves 4.

RICE VENETIAN STYLE

RISO ALLA VENEZIANO

2 cups uncooked rice
1 onion, chopped
½ cup olive oil or butter
3 tablesp. grated Parmesan cheese
3 cups fish or shrimp stock

Wash rice under cold running water, and drain. Brown onion in oil for 3 minutes. Remove onion from pan, and add rice to the same oil. Brown rice over a low flame, stirring constantly. Add 1 cup fish or shrimp stock. Continue cooking over low flame until rice is tender, about 30 minutes. Add the balance of the stock a little at a time. Rice should be moist, but not soupy. Stir constantly to prevent sticking. When rice is tender, stir in cheese and serve immediately. Serves 6 to 8. Rice prepared this way is an excellent accompaniment to fried shrimp or fish.

SPINACH BALLS

SPINNACI POLPETTA

2 cups cooked spinach, chopped
½ cup grated Parmesan cheese
½ lb. ricotta
1 egg
Salt and pepper
1 recipe Plain Tomato Sauce, see p. 61
3 tablesp. grated Parmesan cheese

Drain spinach well. Combine chopped spinach, cheese, ricotta, egg, and seasonings, and mix thoroughly. Shape 1 heaping tablesp. of mixture into a ball, and roll each ball in flour. Drop balls into 3 qts. boiling salted water 5 at a time, and simmer slowly. Cook 5 minutes, counting from the time

that balls rise to surface. Lift balls gently out of water with a slotted spoon, and place them in serving dish. Cover with tomato sauce, and sprinkle with additional cheese. Serve immediately. Serves 4 to 6.
VARIATION: Substitute 6 tablesp. melted butter for tomato sauce.

SWISS CHARD PATTIES

BIETOLE PASTICCETTO

2 cups cooked swiss chard, chopped
1 cup bread crumbs
¼ cup grated Parmesan cheese
1 egg, slightly beaten
Salt and pepper
½ cup olive or salad oil

Drain chopped chard well. Mix thoroughly with crumbs, cheese, egg, and seasonings. Shape into 3 in. patties about ½ in. thick, and fry in hot oil until golden brown on both sides. Serve hot. Serves 4.

STUFFED TOMATOES

POMODORO RIPIENO

6 medium-sized tomatoes
4 anchovy fillets, chopped
1 cup bread crumbs
2 tablesp. grated Parmesan cheese
2 ⅛-in. slices Italian salami, diced
Salt and pepper
¼ cup olive oil
1 teasp. oregano (optional)

Wash tomatoes. With a sharp knife cut a thin slice from the stem end of each tomato, and scoop out pulp and seed gently with a spoon. (Save pulp for soup.) Combine remaining ingredients, divide mixture into 6 parts, and stuff each tomato. Brush bottom of baking pan with 1 tablesp. olive oil. Set tomatoes in pan, and sprinkle top of each tomato with ½ teasp. oil. Bake in moderate oven 350° 30 minutes. Serve hot. Serves 6.

TOMATOES STUFFED WITH MUSHROOMS

POMODORO IMBOTTITO CON FUNGHI

6 large firm tomatoes
3 tablesp. olive oil
½ onion, chopped fine
½ cup mushrooms, sliced thin
2 chicken livers, chopped
1 cup bread crumbs
1 tablesp. grated Parmesan cheese
Salt and pepper
2 eggs, slightly beaten

Wash tomatoes and wipe dry. Cut off a thin slice from the stem end of each tomato, and scoop out pulp and seeds. Saute onion and mushrooms in oil 5 minutes, stirring occasionally. Add livers, and cook 2 minutes longer. Remove from flame, add remaining ingredients, and mix thoroughly. Stuff tomatoes with this mixture. Brush a shallow baking pan with 1 tablesp. olive oil, and set tomatoes upright in pan. Pour an additional ½ teasp. olive oil over each tomato and bake in moderate oven 350° 30 minutes. Serve hot. Serves 6.

GLAZED TURNIPS

RAPE

1 lb. white turnips
3 tablesp. butter
1 teasp. flour
¾ teasp. sugar
Salt and pepper
1 teasp. grated onion
½ cup water or stock

Wash and pare turnips, and cut crosswise into ½ in. slices. Melt butter in frying pan, add turnip slices, and stir until slices are well coated with butter. Combine remaining ingredients, blend well, and pour into pan. Cover pan tightly and cook over low flame until turnips are tender, stirring occasionally. If necessary add liquid during cooking, to prevent scorching. Serve hot. Serves 4.

VEGETABLE CASSEROLE

VEGETALI AL FORNO

1 eggplant
2 large onions, sliced (optional)
1 zucchini
4 fresh tomatoes, sliced
¼ cup olive oil
Salt and pepper
¾ lb. mozzarella cheese, sliced
3 tablesp. chopped fresh basil (optional)

Pare eggplant and cut into ½ in. slices. Cut zucchini into ¼ in. crosswise slices, but do not pare. Grease the bottom of a baking dish with olive oil. Put in a layer of eggplant, a layer of onion, a layer of zucchini, a layer of tomatoes, and a layer of cheese. Repeat until all ingredients are used. Pour olive oil over all, sprinkle with salt and pepper, and bake in a moderate oven 350° until vegetables are tender, and cheese is melted, about 45 minutes. Serve as a main dish for meatless meal. Serves 4.

PICKLED ZUCCHINI

ZUCCHINI ALLA ACETO

2 large zucchini, 2 lbs. each
½ cup olive oil
Salt and pepper
2 sprigs fresh mint or basil, chopped; or, 1 teasp. oregano
1 clove garlic, chopped (optional)
½ cup wine vinegar

Wash zucchini and scrape lightly. Cut crosswise into 1 in. slices, and fry in hot oil until light brown, about 3 minutes. Sprinkle with salt and pepper. Place in layers in an earthenware dish or casserole, and sprinkle each layer with basil and garlic.

Boil vinegar 3 minutes with oil left in frying pan. Pour vinegar over zucchini, and set in refrigerator overnight. Pickled zucchini will keep 2 weeks in refrigerator, and may be served as a side dish with meat, fowl, game, or fish. Enough for 6. NOTE: 1½ tablesp. sugar added to the vinegar will give a sweet and sour pickle.

ZUCCHINI WITH RICE

ZUCCHINI CON RISO

1 cup uncooked rice
1 large zucchini, about 2 lbs.
Salt and pepper
3 tablesp. oil
1 teasp. fresh basil or parsley

Cook rice in boiling salted water until almost tender. While rice is cooking, wash and scrape zucchini lightly. Cut into 1 in. cubes and fry in hot oil over medium flame 10 minutes, until light brown. Add fried zucchini to rice as it is boiling, season with pepper and a very little salt, add basil or parsley, and continue boiling until rice and zucchini are tender. Serve hot. Serves 4.

STUFFED ZUCCHINI

ZUCCHINI IMBOTTITI

3 medium-sized zucchini, ½ lb. each
3 tablesp. olive oil
½ lb. ground veal
2 slices prosciutto, chopped
1 small onion, chopped
1 tablesp. chopped parsley
½ cup canned tomatoes; or, ½ cup stock
½ cup bread crumbs
Salt and pepper

Wash zucchini, but do not peel. Cut into halves lengthwise, scoop out pulp, mash, and put through a food chopper. Saute pulp, ground veal, prosciutto, and onion in oil until meat is lightly browned. Add parsley and tomatoes and cook over medium flame until liquid is absorbed, about 15 minutes, stirring occasionally. Then add crumbs, salt, and pepper. Put zucchini shells in a shallow greased baking dish, and stuff each half-shell with filling. Sprinkle 2 tablesp. olive oil over each shell, and bake in moderate oven 350° until tender. Serve hot. Serves 6.

ZUCCHINI STUFFED WITH TUNA FISH

ZUCCHINI RIPIENI CON TONNA

1 recipe Basic Tomato Sauce, see p. 61
2 medium-sized zucchini, ½ lb. each
2 tablesp. grated Parmesan cheese
1 small onion, grated
1 tablesp. chopped parsley
1 3-oz. can tuna fish in olive oil
Salt and pepper
⅓ cup bread crumbs

Wash zucchini, but do not peel. Slice off about ¼ in. from top and discard. Scoop out pulp with apple corer or potato peeler. Combine remaining ingredients and mix thoroughly. Stuff zucchini with this mixture. Place in deep baking dish, pour Basic Tomato Sauce over zucchini, and bake in moderate oven 375° until tender, 40 to 45 minutes. Serve hot. Serves 4.

VERMICELLI WITH ZUCCHINI: *See p. 44.*

CHAPTER ELEVEN

Salads

HINTS FOR MAKING SALADS

Both appearance and texture must be right if a salad is to be a success. Remove any wilted leaves from salad greens, so that only crisp leaves will be used. (Save wilted leaves, and use them to make soups and stocks.) Wash leafy vegetables well in cold water, but do not soak them. Drain in a colander, or place the leaves on absorbent paper to drain. Greens are most appetizing when they are crisp and dry.

The proper time to mix a salad is about 5 minutes before serving. That way, the leaves will be moist with dressing but not soaked to limpness when you bring the salad to the table. Use a bowl large enough to toss salad without spilling. You may rub the bowl with a cut clove of garlic, if you wish. Place the greens in the bowl, pour the dressing over them, and toss lightly until the leaves are well coated. (Italians prefer to toss salads with the fingers, rather than with a fork and spoon.) Serve immediately.

Following are some excellent combinations for the salad bowl. Serve them tossed with any desired salad dressing. If you choose to rub your salad bowl with garlic, omit any garlic in the dressing. Each of these salads will serve 2 to 4 people.

SUGGESTIONS FOR SALAD BOWLS

1. 1 lb. dandelion greens, in 2 in. pieces
   20 pitted ripe olives

2. ½ head chicory, in 2 in. pieces
   ½ head fresh escarole, in 2 in. pieces
   1 cup fresh dandelion greens, in 2 in. pieces

3. 1 large red onion, sliced
   ½ head lettuce, in 1 in. pieces
   2 large ripe tomatoes, in wedges
   ¼ teasp. oregano

4. ½ head lettuce, in 1 in. pieces
   ½ head chicory, in 2 in. pieces
   1 green pepper, diced

5. 1 cucumber, sliced
   2 scallions, chopped
   ½ head lettuce, in 1 in. pieces
   1 green pepper, diced
   4 radishes, sliced

6. ¼ head escarole, in 1 in. pieces
   ½ head romaine, in 1 in. pieces
   ½ head chicory, in 2 in. pieces
   ¼ head endive, in 2 in. pieces
   1 celery stalk, chopped
   3 scallions, chopped; or, 1 sweet onion, sliced

7. 1 head romaine, in 1 in. pieces
   1 celery stalk, chopped
   1 medium-sized red or sweet onion, sliced
   2 large ripe tomatoes, cut in wedges
   2 hard-boiled eggs, sliced, for garnish

8. 6 large fresh tomatoes, cut in wedges
   3 sprigs fresh basil, chopped.

COMBINATION LETTUCE SALAD

INSALATA MISTA

1 clove garlic, cut in half
1 head lettuce, in 1 in. pieces
1 celery stalk, diced
1 bunch radishes, chopped
1 small cucumber, sliced
1 scallion, chopped
¼ cup olive oil
2 tablesp. wine vinegar
Salt and pepper
2 tomatoes, cut in wedges

Rub salad bowl with garlic. Wash all vegetables, prepare as directed, and combine in salad bowl. Pour on oil, vinegar, and seasonings, and toss with hands. Serves 6.

ESCAROLE SALAD

INSALATA D'ESCAROLA

2 small heads escarole, in 2 in. pieces
Salt and pepper
1 clove garlic, cut in half
¼ cup olive oil
½ cup wine vinegar

Rub salad bowl with garlic. Place escarole in bowl, combine other ingredients, and toss thoroughly. Serves 6.

FENNEL SALAD

INSALATA DI FINOCCHIO

1 lb. fennel
1 head lettuce
3 tablesp. olive oil
1 clove garlic, cut in half
¼ cup wine vinegar
Salt and pepper

Wash vegetables and dice. Rub bowl with garlic. Combine all other ingredients, pour over vegetables, and toss well. Serves 6.

GREEN PEPPER SALAD

INSALATA DI PEPERONI

4 green peppers, diced
¼ cup olive oil
½ cup wine vinegar
Salt and pepper

Combine all ingredients, and toss well. Serves 4.

LETTUCE WITH ORANGE DRESSING

INSALATA D'LETTUGA E ARANCI

1 large head lettuce, in 1 in. pieces
1 tablesp. olive oil
Salt and pepper
Juice of 2 medium-sized oranges

Season lettuce with salt and pepper. Blend oil and orange juice, pour over lettuce, and toss with hands. Serves 6.

ROMAINE GREEN SALAD

INSALATA D'VERDE E ROMANA

1 head romaine, in 1 in. pieces
2 green peppers, diced
2 celery stalks with leaves, diced
1 small head escarole, in 1 in. pieces
3 tablesp. olive oil
6 tablesp. wine vinegar
Salt and pepper

Combine all ingredients, and toss well with hands. Serves 6.

TOSSED SALAD

INSALATA

1 medium-sized head of lettuce, in 1 in. pieces
1 clove garlic, cut in half
1 2-oz. can anchovy fillets with capers
¼ cup olive oil
¼ cup wine vinegar
8 black or green olives, whole
1 tablesp. oregano
Salt and pepper

Rub salad bowl with garlic. Combine lettuce, anchovies, the oil from the anchovy can, olive oil, vinegar, olives, oregano, and a very little salt and pepper. Toss with fingers lightly until well blended. Serves 4.

Dressings for Green Salads

ANCHOVY SALAD DRESSING

CONDIMENTO DI ACCIUGHE

4 anchovy fillets
½ cup olive oil
3 tablesp. wine vinegar
Pinch of pepper

Pound anchovies to a paste in mortar. Add remaining ingredients, and mix well. Serve with tomatoes or any green salad. This dressing should be made to serve immediately, as it will only keep for 2 days at the most. Store in refrigerator, if necessary, and shake well before using. Makes ⅝ cup.

ITALIAN CHEESE DRESSING

CONDIMENTO DI FORMAGGIO

½ cup olive oil
3 tablesp. wine vinegar
Salt and pepper
¼ cup grated cheese

Combine all ingredients and blend well. Place in a jar and store in refrigerator. Shake well before using. Good on escarole, cucumbers, romaine, or green peppers. Makes ¾ cup.

ITALIAN DRESSING

CONDIMENTO DI ITALIANA

⅓ cup wine vinegar
1 clove garlic
6 tablesp. olive oil
Salt and pepper
Pinch of oregano or dried basil

Combine all ingredients in a jar, and shake well. Let stand overnight in refrigerator. Shake well before using. Serve with lettuce, cucumbers, leftover soup meat, or fish. Makes ½ cup.

SALAD DRESSING

2 cups wine vinegar
¾ cup olive oil
2 whole garlic cloves

Combine all ingredients in jar, shake well, and store in refrigerator till needed. Makes 2¾ cups.

Main Dish Salads

EGG SALAD

INSALATA DI UOVA

6 hard-boiled eggs
¼ cup minced onion
¼ cup diced celery
2 tablesp. olive oil
1 tablesp. wine vinegar
Salt and pepper

Slice hard-boiled eggs and arrange on serving dish. Combine remaining ingredients, pour over eggs, and garnish with parsley. Serves 4.

HUNTER'S SALAD

INSALATA CACCIATORA

2 cups canned kidney beans with chili sauce
2 hard-boiled eggs, sliced
5 scallions, sliced
2 medium-sized tomatoes, cut in wedges
2 tablesp. chopped green pepper
2 cooked potatoes, diced
½ cup diced cucumbers
3 radishes, diced
½ cup wine vinegar
¼ cup olive oil
Salt and pepper

Combine all ingredients, mixing well. This salad will keep indefinitely in a refrigerator. Serve as a main dish with Italian bread. Serves 6.

LOBSTER SALAD: *See p. 102.*

OCTOPUS SALAD: *See p. 104.*

OLIVE SALAD

INSALATA CON OLIVE

¼ lb. green Italian olives, pitted
¼ lb. black Italian olives, pitted
5 pickled green peppers, cut in eighths
½ cup celery, diced
¼ cup olive oil
1 large onion, sliced
1 tablesp. oregano
¼ cup wine vinegar
Salt and pepper

Combine all ingredients, and mix well. This may be used as an antipasto, salad, or condiment with fish and pork. Keeps well in refrigerator. Serves 6.

ITALIAN POTATO SALAD

INSALATA PATATE

6 medium-sized cooked potatoes
1 small onion, finely chopped
¼ cup chopped parsley
¼ cup olive oil
½ cup wine vinegar
Salt and pepper

Cut potatoes into ½ in. slices. Combine remaining ingredients, pour over potatoes, and toss well. Serves 6 to 8.

SHRIMP SALAD

INSALATA DI GAMBERI

2 lbs. medium-sized shrimp
¼ cup olive oil
2 tablesp. chopped parsley
Salt and pepper

Boil shrimp in salted water 5 minutes, until bright pink. Cool, drain, shell, and de-vein. Toss in a salad bowl with remaining ingredients. Serve hot or cold. Serves 6.
NOTE: Canned shrimp may be used in this salad.

STRING BEAN SALAD

INSALATA DI FAGIOLINI

1 lb. string beans
¼ cup olive oil
6 tablesp. wine vinegar
Salt and pepper

Wash beans, cut off ends and strings. Cook in small amount of boiling salted water until tender. Do not overcook. Drain, cool, and toss in salad bowl with remaining ingredients. Serves 4.

TOMATO SALAD

INSALATA DI POMODORO

6 tomatoes, cut in wedges
1 large onion, sliced
2 tablesp. olive oil
1 tablesp. water
1 teasp. oregano
Salt and pepper

Combine all ingredients in salad bowl, and toss lightly. Serves 4.

TOMATO SALAD #2

INSALATA DI POMODORO

6 tomatoes, cut in wedges
½ cup olive oil
Juice of 2 lemons
¼ cup basil
Salt and pepper

Arrange tomatoes in serving dish. Combine remaining ingredients, and pour over tomatoes. Serves 6.

TUNA FISH SALAD: *See p. 114.*

CHAPTER TWELVE

Bread and Pizza

Bread (Pane)

HINTS FOR MAKING BREAD

FOLLOW THE RECIPE CAREFULLY. SIFT THE FLOUR BEFORE measuring. Use a good grade of yeast, and make sure it is fresh. If you use dry yeast, check the expiration date on the package. Compressed yeast should be creamy white, and crumble easily. Both types of yeast must be kept under refrigeration until used.

Heap all dry ingredients in a deep pan or bowl, or on a bread board or table top. Make a well in them with your fist. Test water by putting a few drops on your wrist; if the water feels neither hot nor cold, but lukewarm, it is right. Pour the water into the well, and stir or crumble the yeast in it until the yeast is well dissolved.

Knead bread for ten minutes. Kneading is a very important procedure, for without it the bread cannot have a smooth grain. To knead: Flatten dough out slightly. Then pick up the edge farthest away from you, fold it into the rest of the dough, and push lightly with the heel of your palm. Turn the dough slightly on the board or table top, and repeat. When you have kneaded enough the dough will no longer be sticky, and will have a wonderfully satiny feel.

Cover kneaded dough with a towel, and let it rise in a

warm place (85 to 90°) away from any draft. Dough is finished rising when it has doubled in bulk. Do not let the dough rise beyond this point, as it will make a tough bread if you do. Test by pressing gently with a finger tip in the center. If your finger leaves a slight dent which does not disappear, then the dough has risen enough. Punch it down with your wrist, turning the dough towards you. Let it rise a second time until doubled in bulk.

Cut dough into parts, allowing one part for each loaf. Flatten each part out, which will help to press out some of the air bubbles. Shape into desired loaves, and place loaves in well-greased bread pans. Cover with a cloth, and again let rise until doubled in bulk. When your finger leaves a slight dent in the bread, it is ready to bake. Preheat the oven to moderate, or 350°. Place loaves in the center of the oven, and bake until brown. Test for doneness by tapping the bottom of the loaf. If the bread sounds hollow, it is done.

BASIC BREAD RECIPE

RICETTA FONDAMENTALE

10 cups flour, sifted
2¼ cups lukewarm water
2 pkgs. dried or compressed yeast
2 teasp. salt
¼ cup salad oil

Sift flour into bowl or on to large bread board. Make a well in center of flour and put water, yeast, and salt into it. Crumble yeast in water until it is well dissolved. Mix with hands. Knead thoroughly, about 10 minutes, until dough is smooth and elastic. Pour oil over dough, and continue to knead until dough is no longer sticky, about 5 minutes. Cover dough with clean towel and let it rise in a warm place away from drafts, until doubled in bulk. Test by pressing with finger tip; if your finger leaves an indentation which does not disappear, the dough has risen enough. Divide dough into 2 parts. Roll each into an oblong loaf. Starting with the wide side, roll the loaves back and forth until they are 12 in. long. Place loaves on ungreased baking sheet about 5 in. apart. Make 3 diagonal cuts on each loaf with a sharp knife, or 1 lengthwise cut. Cover with a clean towel and let rise in a warm place until doubled in bulk, about 1 hour. Preheat oven to 425°, and bake loaves at this heat 10 minutes. Reduce oven temperature to 375° and bake until loaves are golden brown and sound hollow when tapped, about 30 minutes. Cool on a rack. Makes 2 loaves.

NOTE: This recipe may be used for pizza dough, see p. 184.

VARIATIONS: 1. If a chewy crust is desired, brush the top of the bread lightly with a pastry brush dipped in warm water before putting loaves in the oven. After the bread is baked, brush again with warm water and put loaves on a rack to cool.

2. The loaves may be coated with sesame seeds. Use ¼ cup seeds, and put them on a flat plate. After bread has been shaped into loaves, roll them back and forth on the plate so that the seeds cover the entire surface. For a chewy crust, brush lightly with warm water, then roll in sesame.
3. St. Joseph's Bread: Add ¼ cup anise seeds to dough with water and yeast. Shape into 2 round loaves, or into the shape of a long beard, symbolic of St. Joseph's beard. Brush loaves with mixture of 1 egg yolk diluted with 1 tablesp. water before baking. Sprinkle a little cornmeal on the bottom of the baking pan, and bake as directed. This is the traditional St. Joseph's Bread, and is blessed with the rest of the food at the Festa di San Giuseppe on March 19th.
4. Substitute 3 tablesp. lard for salad oil. Soften it to room temperature, and add with water and yeast.
5. Cut hot loaves in two lengthwise, and sprinkle 2 tablesp. oil on each half. Sprinkle with salt and pepper and press the 2 halves together gently. Serve immediately.

6. To use left-over bread dough, roll ¼ in. thick, and cut with 2 in. cookie cutter. Dot circles with tiny pieces of mozzarella cheese, cover with another dough circle, and fry in hot oil until they puff up and become golden brown. Drain on unglazed paper and serve hot.
7. Bread sticks: Pinch off pieces of risen dough the size of a walnut. Roll balls into long strips the thickness of a pencil. Round off edges, lay on greased cookie sheet, let rise until doubled in bulk, and brush with egg white or milk. Roll in coarse salt, and bake in a moderate oven 350° until golden brown, about 12 minutes.
8. Italian Raised Doughnuts: Use left-over bread dough and roll ½ in. thick. Cut into 2 in. squares or rounds. Let rise only 10 minutes, then fry in hot oil until dough puffs up and becomes golden brown, about 5 minutes. Drain on unglazed paper and sprinkle with granulated sugar. Serve immediately.
9. Rolls with Italian Sausage: Roll left-over dough ½ in. thick. Cut into 3 in. rounds or squares. Place dots of sausage on one round, cover with another round, and fold the top round under the bottom to hold the two together. Place on a greased pan, and let rise until doubled in bulk, about 30 minutes. Bake in preheated hot oven 400° until brown, about 15 minutes. Serve hot.

BOLOGNA BREAD

½ cup milk
⅓ cup butter
⅓ cup sugar
1 cup yellow corn meal
1½ teasp. baking powder
½ teasp. salt
½ cup flour
¼ cup currants or seedless raisins
¼ cup chopped nuts
1 tablesp. candied orange peel, chopped
1 egg

Scald milk. Add butter, blend well, and cool. Mix the sugar, corn meal, flour, baking powder, salt, currants, and orange peel on a board or table top. Make a well in these ingredients, and pour in the cooled scalded milk. Add egg. Knead the dough into a firm smooth ball, about 3 minutes. If dough is too sticky, add a little more flour. Divide dough into 2 portions, and flatten each with a rolling pin until it is ¼ in. thick. Shape each loaf to fit a 9-in. pie plate. Grease 2 9-in. pie plates, and put dough into them. Brush tops with slightly beaten egg yolk, and bake in moderate oven 350° until bread shrinks from side of pan, about 25 to 30 minutes. Bread will be a flat loaf when done. Makes 2 loaves.

EASTER BREAD

CRESCA

8 cups sifted flour
1 teasp. salt
1 teasp. pepper
1½ cups grated Parmesan cheese
¾ cup lukewarm milk or water
2 pkgs. of dried or compressed yeast
6 eggs, well beaten
¼ cup olive oil

Sift dry ingredients together on to a bread board. Make a well in the center, and pour milk, yeast, eggs, and olive oil into it. Knead dough until smooth and elastic, about 10 minutes. Add enough flour to make a stiff dough, if necessary. Cover and let rise in warm place until doubled in bulk, about 2 hours. Punch dough down. Cover and let rise again until doubled in bulk, about 30 minutes. Turn dough out on bread board, and shape into round loaf to fit a 9-in. pie pan. Cover and let rise 6 hours. Bake in moderate oven 350° for 1 hour, until loaf sounds hollow when tapped. Makes 2 loaves. This is the traditional Easter bread in certain parts of Northern Italy.

GARLIC BREAD

PANE DI AGLIO

1 long loaf Italian bread
2 cloves garlic
½ cup olive oil
Salt and pepper

Cut loaf into ½ in. slices and toast in hot oven until lightly brown. Crush garlic in garlic press, add oil, salt, and pepper, and blend well. Brush over hot slices of toast, and serve as antipasto or with any green salad.

LIGURIAN BREAD

PANE DI LIGURE

I.

1 cake compressed yeast, or 1 envelope dried yeast
½ cup lukewarm water
1 cup flour
1 tablesp. sugar
1 tablesp. olive oil
1 tablesp. melted butter
1 egg
1 cup flour

Dissolve yeast in water, place in a large bowl and add sifted flour. Beat thoroughly, cover, and let rise in a warm place overnight. Next morning add sugar, olive oil, butter, egg, and an additional cup of sifted flour. Knead well, cover, and let rise in a warm place until doubled in bulk, about 2 hours. When it has risen, prepare the following things:

II.

1 tablesp. anise seed
¼ cup red wine
¼ cup marsala or sherry

Combine these ingredients and let stand.

III.

7 tablesp. sugar
1 tablesp. olive oil
2 tablesp. melted butter
5 eggs
3 cups sifted flour

Combine these ingredients and add to I after it has risen. Then add II. If dough is too soft and sticky, add more flour to make a stiff dough. Knead about 10 minutes. Cover and let rise in a warm place until doubled in bulk, about 2 hours. Punch down, and let rise again until doubled in bulk, about ½ hour. Shape into a round loaf, place in a greased 12-in. pie pan, cover, and let rise until doubled in bulk, about 1½ hours. A few minutes before baking, brush with egg yolk diluted with a tablesp. of orange juice. Bake in moderate oven 375° 1 to 1½ hours. Makes 1 large loaf.
NOTE: This is a solid bread with a good flavor. The dough will rise slowly.

LITTLE MUFFINS

STIACCIATA

½ cup lukewarm water
1 pkg. compressed or dried yeast
1 tablesp. sugar
½ teasp. salt
½ cup flour
1 cup butter
3 eggs
2½ cups sifted flour
¼ cup confectioners sugar
2 egg yolks, well beaten

Dissolve yeast in lukewarm water. Combine yeast, sugar, and salt in deep bowl, and add ½ cup sifted flour to make a sponge. Stir well until smooth, cover, and let rise in a warm place until doubled in bulk, about 40 minutes.

Cream butter, add eggs one at a time, and beat well. Sift 2½ cups flour on to a board, and make a well in the center.

Put risen sponge into well, and knead dough thoroughly, about 5 to 7 minutes, until smooth and elastic. Put in greased bowl, cover, and let rise until doubled in bulk, about 2½ hours.

Grease 24 large muffin cups with butter. Pinch off pieces of dough the size of a walnut, and roll into balls. Put in muffin cups. With a spoon make a cavity in each ball, and put another ball into it the size of a filbert. Cover with cloth and let rise in a warm place 30 minutes. Brush tops with egg yolk and dust lightly with confectioners sugar. Bake in hot oven 425° until golden brown, 30 minutes. Test for doneness by inserting toothpick into center of muffin. If the toothpick comes out clean, the muffins are done. Remove from pan and cool on rack. The muffins may be sprinkled with more confectioners sugar if desired. Makes about 2 dozen.

NEAPOLITAN BREAD

PANE DI NAPOLETANA

3⅓ cups pastry flour
1 lb. almond meal (finely ground almonds)
1 cup sugar
Grated rind of 1 lemon
Grated rind of 1 orange
1 cup butter
5 egg yolks
1 egg yolk, slightly beaten

Combine flour, almond meal, sugar, lemon and orange rinds, and butter on a bread board. Mix lightly with fingers until mixture resembles coarse cornmeal. Add 5 egg yolks and knead well for 10 minutes. Roll the dough to the size and shape of a rolling pin, wrap in waxed paper, and chill for 1 hour in refrigerator. Then, cut dough *lengthwise* with a sharp knife into 6 equal slices. Braid 3 of the strips together loosely and press ends together to seal. Repeat with other 3 strips. Place loaves 3 inches apart on greased cookie sheet, and brush each loaf with slightly beaten egg yolk. Bake in moderate oven 350° until a delicate brown, about 1 hour.

Remove from oven and cool on rack. Serve slices with wine. Makes 2 loaves.

NORTHERN CHESTNUT BREAD

PANE DI CASTAGNA

⅔ cup chestnut puree (about ½ lb. chestnuts)
½ cup figs, cut into small pieces
½ cup white raisins
⅓ cup currants
⅔ cup brandy, rum, sherry, or marsala
½ cup blanched almonds, chopped
1¼ cups chestnut flour; or, 1¼ cups cake flour
3 tablesp. olive oil

Combine figs, raisins, currants, and brandy. Let stand for 30 minutes. Add chestnut puree, chopped almonds, and flour. Knead until mixture holds together, adding more flour if dough is too soft and sticky, and more brandy if dough seems too dry. Grease a 9-in. heavy frying pan with 2 tablesp. olive oil. Put dough in frying pan and mold into round loaf. Brush top with balance of oil. Bake in slow oven 250° until bread sounds hollow when tapped, about 1¼ to 1½ hours. Makes 1 loaf. This bread is very popular among Northern Italian peasants, and can be made whenever chestnuts are available. It has a good flavor which improves if the loaf is kept for 24 hours before serving.

SICILIAN ROLLS

GUASTELLE

1 cup water
¼ cup oil
2 tablesp. sugar
1½ teasp. salt
¼ cup lukewarm water
1 pkg. dried or compressed yeast
1 egg
3 cups sifted flour

Heat 1 cup water, and add oil, sugar and salt. Cool to lukewarm. Dissolve yeast in ¼ cup lukewarm water, and add to cooled mixture. Blend in 1 egg. Gradually add 3 cups sifted flour. Do not knead. Shape dough on floured board into rolls, using any shape desired. Place rolls on greased pan or cookie sheet, and let rise in a warm place until doubled in bulk, about 1 hour. Bake in moderate oven 375° 15 to 20 minutes, until golden brown. Cool on rack. Makes about 15 rolls.

Pizza

Pizza IS A GENERAL TERM MEANING THAT WHICH IS FLAT, ROUND, and baked, like a pie. It is a popular term today for a light crunchy breadstuff which is served topped with any one of an amazing variety of aromatic baked-on fillings.

Experimenting in my own kitchen I have discovered that pizza dough may be spread with any desired filling and then frozen successfully in the refrigerator or deep freeze for at least a week. To bake frozen pizza, omit the 10 minute rising period and leave it in the oven 30 minutes instead of 25. The extra 5 minutes allows it to thaw and rise in the oven.

MAMA MIA BASIC PIZZA DOUGH

1 pkg. dried or compressed yeast
1⅓ cups lukewarm water
2 tablesp. salad, olive, or peanut oil
1 teasp. salt
4 cups sifted flour

Dissolve yeast in lukewarm water. Add oil. Sift flour and salt into bowl, add yeast mixture, and knead until

smooth, about 10 minutes. Cover with clean towel and let rise in warm place until doubled in bulk, about 2 hours. Oil an 11 by 15 baking sheet, or 2 12-in. pie pans with 2 tablesp. olive oil. Pat and stretch risen dough to fill pans, pushing dough well into corners of pan. Spread filling on top of dough and allow to rise 10 minutes. (If pizza has been frozen, omit this rising.) Bake in hot oven 400° until pizza is golden brown, about 25 minutes. Lift pizza slightly with broad spatula to see if bottom is sufficiently brown. Remove from oven, and serve immediately in pan.
NOTE: The basic recipe for Italian Bread, see p. 175, may also be used as a pizza dough.

MAMA MIA FAMOUS PIZZA

MAMA MIA FAMOSO PIZZA

1 recipe Mama Mia Pizza Dough
2 medium-sized onions, sliced thin
¼ cup olive oil
1 2-oz. can anchovy fillets
1 6-oz. can tomato paste
3 cups water
Salt and pepper (use very little salt)
1 teasp. oregano
2 tablesp. olive oil
½ cup grated Romano or Parmesan cheese

Saute onions in oil until light brown, stirring occasionally. Add anchovies and oil from anchovy can. Stir constantly until anchovies are dissolved. Add tomato paste and water, and stir until well blended. Add seasonings and oregano, and simmer uncovered until mixture is thick, about 1 hour, stirring occasionally. Grease the bottom of an 11 by 15 baking pan, and pat and stretch pizza dough to fit, pushing dough well into corners. Spread filling on top and allow to rise for 10 minutes. Sprinkle with cheese and bake in moderate oven 375° until pizza is golden brown, about 30 minutes. Serve immediately. 4 medium servings.

VARIATIONS:

1. MOZZARELLA CHEESE TOPPING

¾ lb. mozzarella cheese, coarsely grated
1 #2 can tomatoes, drained
1 medium-sized onion
Salt and pepper

Spread grated cheese evenly on dough in pan. Place drained tomatoes in a bowl. Grate onion on coarse side of grater directly into tomatoes. Blend well and spread over cheese. Sprinkle with salt and pepper and bake as directed.

2. SAUSAGE TOPPING

1 lb. Italian sweet sausage, cut into ½ in. pieces; or, 1 lb. bulk sausage
1 onion, chopped
½ 6-oz. can tomato paste
1½ cups water
½ cup grated Parmesan cheese
Salt and pepper
Pinch of oregano

Brown sausage and onion in frying pan, turning occasionally. Blend tomato paste and water. Pour into sausage and simmer 10 minutes. Pour over dough and sprinkle with seasonings, cheese, and oregano. Bake as directed.

. . . .

ANCHOVY PIZZA

1 2-oz. can anchovy fillets
2 tablesp. olive oil
2 onions, sliced thin
1 #2 can tomatoes
¼ cup grated Parmesan or provolone cheese
Salt and pepper
1 recipe Basic Pizza Dough, *see p. 183*

Drain the oil from the anchovies, combine it with olive oil, and saute onions in this oil until soft. Add tomatoes which have been mashed with fork, and simmer uncovered 15 minutes, stirring occasionally. Spread dough on greased baking sheet, and cover with anchovies which have been cut in pieces. Spread cooked tomato sauce over anchovies, sprinkle with cheese, salt and pepper, and let rise 5 minutes. Bake until golden brown in hot oven 400°. Serve at once. Serves 4.

COMBINATION FILLING FOR PIZZA

1 recipe Basic Pizza Dough, see p. 183
1 tablesp. olive oil
1 small onion, sliced
½ 6-oz. can tomato paste
1½ cups water
¼ lb. Italian sweet sausage, cut fine
1 strip bacon, diced
1 tablesp. minced green pepper
¼ cup canned sliced mushrooms
¼ lb. mozzarella cheese, diced
Salt and pepper
Pinch of oregano (optional)

Saute onion in oil until soft. Add tomato paste and water, and stir until well blended. Simmer uncovered 20 minutes. While sauce is cooking spread dough on greased baking sheet, and cover with all ingredients except seasonings. Add cooked sauce, and sprinkle with salt, pepper, and oregano. Bake in hot oven 400° until golden brown. Serve immediately. Serves 4.

PIZZA WITH EGGS

PIZZA CON UOVA

1 recipe Basic Pizza Dough, see p. 183
4 hard-boiled eggs, shelled and halved
3 tablesp. olive oil
Salt and pepper

Spread dough on greased baking sheet. Make 8 depressions in dough, and insert ½ hard-boiled egg in each depression.

Spread dough over eggs so that they are covered as completely as possible. Brush top surface with oil, sprinkle with salt and pepper, and bake in moderate oven until golden brown. Serve hot. Serves 4.

PIZZA MARCIANA

1 recipe Basic Pizza Dough, see p. 183
¼ cup olive oil
1 tablesp. rosemary
¼ teasp. salt
½ teasp. pepper

Spread dough on greased cookie sheet, and pour oil over surface. Sprinkle with rosemary, salt, and pepper, and bake in moderate oven 375° until golden brown. Serve immediately. Serves 4.

MUSHROOM PIZZA

1 #2½ can tomatoes
¼ cup canned sliced mushrooms
1 medium onion, sliced thin
12 slices mozzarella cheese
¼ cup grated Parmesan or Romano cheese
1 teasp. oregano
Salt and pepper
½ lb. Italian sausage in bulk
1 teasp. olive oil
1 recipe Basic Pizza Dough, see p. 183

Spread dough on greased baking sheet, and cover with tomatoes which have been mashed with a fork. Make depressions in dough and put mushrooms in them. Spread onions and sliced mozzarella on top, sprinkle with grated cheese and seasonings, spread sausage over all, and sprinkle olive oil on top. Bake in hot oven 400° until golden brown. Serve immediately. Serves 4.

CHAPTER THIRTEEN

Cakes, Fillings, Frostings, and Sauces

ABRUIZZI BLACK CAKE

TORTA NERO ALLA ABRUIZZI

4 ozs. (4 sqs.) unsweetened chocolate
½ cup butter
½ cup sugar
3 eggs, separated
¾ cup chopped filberts
⅝ cup flour

Melt chocolate over hot water. Cream butter, add sugar, and continue beating until creamy. Add egg yolks and beat until well blended. Add melted, cooled chocolate, and beat well for 2 minutes. Beat egg whites until stiff but not dry. Fold into chocolate mixture. Combine nuts and sifted flour and fold gently into batter. Pour into an 8-in. square pan lined with waxed paper, and bake in moderate oven 350° until a toothpick inserted into cake comes out clean and cake shrinks from side of pan, 35 to 40 minutes. Cool cake in pan, and frost with Chocolate Frosting, see p. 202.

BABA A RUM

BABA AL RUM

1 pkg. dried or compressed yeast
½ cup lukewarm milk
¾ cup sifted flour
½ cup butter
6 tablesp. sugar
3 eggs
½ teasp. salt
¾ cup currants
1¼ cups sifted flour

Soften yeast in lukewarm milk. Add ¾ cup sifted flour and beat well until smooth. Cover and set in a warm place until sponge has doubled in bulk.

Cream butter and sugar, and add eggs one at a time, beating well after each addition. Add salt, currants, and risen sponge. Blend thoroughly. Add 1¼ cups sifted flour gradually, and beat well.

Grease 12 large muffin cups and fill with dough. Brush top of each muffin with melted butter. Cover and let rise in warm place until doubled in bulk, 1½ hours. Bake in moderate oven 350° 25 minutes. Remove from pan immediately and cool on cake rack. Pour rum sauce over babas 15 minutes before serving. 12 babas.

RUM SAUCE:

¼ cup sugar | *½ cup water*
6 tablesp. light rum

Boil water and sugar over medium flame 5 minutes. Cool for 10 minutes and add rum. Blend well, and pour over babas.

CHESTNUT TORTE: *See p. 252.*

CHRISTMAS EVE CAKE

TORTA VIGILIA DI NATALE

1 cup water
1 cup seedless raisins or currants
¼ cup chopped walnuts
¼ cup chopped pecans
1 cup sugar
½ cup butter
1 egg
2 teasp. vanilla or rum flavoring
1 teasp. baking powder
½ cup sifted flour

Simmer raisins or currants and nut meats in water 5 minutes. Cool. Cream butter and sugar, add egg, and beat well.

Add flavoring and blend. Sift baking powder and flour together, and add to creamed mixture. Beat until well blended. Add cooled fruits, and stir well. Pour into greased 8-in. square pan and bake at 350° 25 minutes. Cool, remove from pan, and cut into squares. This cake keeps well.

SICILIAN CREAM TART

CASSATA ALLA SICILIANA

1 sponge cake, 9-in., see p. 196
1½ lb. ricotta
6 tablesp. rum
½ cup confectioners sugar
2 oz. grated sweet chocolate
¼ cup chopped candied cherries
½ teasp. cinnamon
½ cup chopped toasted almonds

Slice cake into 3 layers. Or, use a commercial sponge cake which may be bought in layers. Sprinkle layers with rum. Crush ricotta very fine with hands or potato masher, add sugar, and beat 3 minutes, until creamy. Stir in remaining ingredients until well blended. Spread over sponge cake layers, using a half-inch of filling on each layer. Spread top and sides with the following frosting:

¼ cup butter
2½ cups confectioners sugar
2 egg whites
1 teasp. almond extract

Cream butter with 1 cup sifted confectioners sugar. Beat egg whites until stiff, and gradually beat into egg whites the remaining 1½ cups confectioners sugar. Fold egg whites into butter mixture, and add the almond extract.

Cover sides and top of cassata evenly with this frosting. Store in refrigerator until ready to serve. Serves 10.

FRUIT CAKE AGRIGENTO

PANFORTE DI AGRIGENTO

5 cups cake flour
2 cups butter
2⅓ cups sugar
10 eggs
2 jiggers rum, brandy, or anisette liqueur
½ lb. mixed candied orange and lemon peel, chopped fine

Sift flour once, measure, and resift 3 times. Cream butter and sugar until light. Add eggs one at a time, beating well after each addition. Add rum and blend well. Add flour ½ cup at a time. Beat until thoroughly mixed.

Grease two 5 by 9 by 3 in. loaf pans and line with waxed paper. Pour batter into pans ½ in. deep and place a layer of fruit on top of batter. Alternate batter and fruit in both pans until they are filled. Bake at 300° for 1¾ hours until golden brown. There will be a narrow crack in the center of each loaf. Remove cake from oven, and invert pans on rack to cool. Do not remove bottom waxed paper until cake is thoroughly cold. Then wrap in waxed paper and store in covered container. This cake may be served cut into 1 in. slices and sprinkled with rum, brandy, or sherry. Serves 8 to 12.

SIENA FRUIT CAKE

PANFORTE DI SIENA

½ cup cake flour
3 tablesp. cocoa
1 teasp. cinnamon
½ teasp. ground allspice
½ teasp. ground nutmeg
½ cup sugar
½ cup honey
¼ lb. almonds
¼ lb. candied fruit, cut fine
½ cup candied lemon and orange peel, cut fine

Sift flour, measure, and resift 3 times with cocoa and spices. Boil honey and sugar in a saucepan 3 minutes over medium flame, stirring constantly. Remove from heat, add nuts and dry ingredients, and stir quickly. Immediately pour into a greased 9-in. square pan which has been lined with waxed paper. Bake in slow oven 300° until cake shrinks from side of pan, about 30 minutes. Cool on rack, and sprinkle top generously with confectioners sugar. Serves 8 to 10. This cake keeps very well in an airtight container.

GENOA TORTE

TORTA DI GENOVESE

6 eggs
1 cup sugar
1 teasp. grated lemon rind
1 teasp. grated orange rind
1⅓ cups cake flour

Beat eggs until light and fluffy. Gradually add sugar and beat well. Add lemon and orange rinds and continue beating until thick and lemon colored. Fold in sifted flour 2 tablesp. at a time. Pour mixture into 9 by 13 cake pan. Bake in moderate 350° oven until cake shrinks from side of pan, 25 to 30 minutes. Frost with Apricot Frosting, see p. 202.

MARGHERITA CAKE

5 eggs, separated
½ cup confectioners sugar
1 tablesp. lemon juice
¼ teasp. almond extract
½ cup potato flour
½ teasp. vanilla extract

Beat egg yolks until thick and lemon colored. Add sugar gradually, and beat for about 5 minutes. Add lemon juice and almond flavoring. Fold in sifted flour. Beat egg whites until they hold a peak, and fold them into yolks. Grease a 10-in. square cake pan, and sprinkle the bottom with confectioners sugar. Pour batter into pan and sprinkle top with additional confectioners sugar. Bake in moderate oven 375° 30 minutes. Cool on a wire rack, and sprinkle vanilla extract over cake. Serves 6 to 8. This recipe makes a crisp, sweet sponge-type cake.

MILANESE CAKE

PANETTONE

1 pkg. dry or compressed yeast
1 cup sugar
¼ cup lukewarm water
4 eggs
¼ cup lukewarm milk
1 cup melted butter
5 cups cake flour
¼ teasp. salt
½ cup candied citron peel, chopped
⅔ cup seedless raisins
¼ cup chopped almonds

All ingredients must be at room temperature. The cake has to be prepared the day before it is to be baked.

Crumble yeast with ½ cup sugar, and add ¼ cup lukewarm water. Let rise until light and bubbly. When sponge has risen, beat eggs slightly with lukewarm milk. Cream melted butter and remaining ½ cup sugar. Combine sifted flour, salt, candied fruit, and raisins, and add to creamed mixture. Stir well, and gradually add beaten eggs. Blend well and stir in yeast sponge. Beat until dough is smooth. Pour into a greased 9-in. tube pan, or into 2 loaf pans, filling them ¾ full. Sprinkle chopped almonds on top of batter, and let rise overnight in a warm place. Bake in a moderate oven 375° next day, about 1 hour. Serve with coffee or wine. Serves 10.

PANCAKE

CASTAGNOCCIO

1½ cups chestnut flour
¼ teasp. salt
2 tablesp. olive oil
1½ cups boiling water
2 tablesp. currants
2 tablesp. seedless raisins
¼ teasp. rosemary
2 tablesp. pine nuts

Preheat oven to 375°. Mix flour, salt, oil, and boiling water, and stir well until smooth. Fold in currants and raisins. Pour batter into a 9-in. pie pan, sprinkle with rosemary and pine nuts, and bake at 375° until top is crisp, about 45 minutes. Slice and serve hot. Serves 6.

ITALIAN RUM CAKE

ZUPPA INGLESE

1 sponge cake, see p. 196; or, use 10 in. sponge cake from bakery.

FILLING:

½ cup sugar
¼ cup cornstarch
⅛ teasp. salt
2½ cups milk
2 eggs, slightly beaten
1 tablesp. rum
1 teasp. vanilla
2 tablesp. creme de cacao
⅔ cup marsala
½ cup light rum
½ pt. whipping cream
2 tablesp. candied fruit, chopped fine

Combine sugar, cornstarch, and salt in top of double boiler. Add ½ cup milk and stir until smooth. Add remainder of milk and cook over hot water until thick and smooth, stirring constantly. Pour small amount of hot mixture on slightly beaten eggs, stir well, and return to double boiler.

Cook 5 minutes more, stirring constantly. Cool custard and divide it into 3 parts. Add the 1 tablesp. rum to one part, the vanilla to the second, and the creme de cacao to the third. Cut cake into 4 layers, and put one layer on serving plate. Mix the marsala and ½ cup of light rum, and pour ¼ cup of this mixture over first layer of cake. Spread with one of the custard mixtures. Repeat with 2nd and 3rd layers, using ¼ cup wine-rum mixture and 1 filling for each layer. Put final, fourth layer on top, and pour remaining ¼ cup wine-rum mixture over it. Refrigerate overnight. At serving time whip cream until stiff. Spread it over top and sides of cake, sprinkle with candied fruit, and serve immediately. Serves 12.

RUM CAKE PALERMO STYLE

TORTA DI RUM ALLA PALERMITANO

1 plain cake or sponge cake
1 cup dark rum, approximately
4 egg yolks
2 tablesp. sugar
½ cup marsala or sherry

Cut cake into 3 layers. Beat egg yolks in top of double boiler 4 minutes, add sugar, and beat 1 minute longer. Add wine and beat until well blended. Cook over hot, never boiling, water, beating constantly, until eggs begin to thicken, about 5 minutes. Remove from flame and beat until frothy. Set aside to cool. When cooled completely, fill cake in the following manner: sprinkle each layer of cake with ⅓ cup dark rum; spread ⅓ of filling on each layer, and put them together. Place in refrigerator and chill 1 hour. Serves 10. This cake may be covered with whipped cream, if desired; in any case, it must be eaten with a spoon.

SPONGE CAKE

PAN DI SPAGNA

6 eggs, separated
½ cup sugar
1½ tablesp. lemon juice
1½ tablesp. grated orange rind
2 tablesp. sherry; or, 1 teasp. almond extract
1 cup cake flour
½ teasp. salt

Have ingredients at room temperature at least an hour before baking.

Beat egg yolks until thick and lemon colored. Beat in sugar, lemon juice, orange rind, and sherry. Beat until foamy. Sift flour 3 times and fold into egg yolks gently but thoroughly. Beat egg whites until foamy, add salt, and beat until stiff but not dry. Fold into yolks. Pour batter into ungreased spring form pan and bake in moderate oven 350° 50 to 60 minutes. Test by pressing lightly with finger tip; if cake springs back at once, it is done. Leave cake in pan to cool, and invert on wire rack. Remove from pan after thoroughly cooled, and if desired, sprinkle the top with brandy or rum and powdered sugar.

SWEETHEART CHEEK

BOCCA DI DAMA

¼ cup almond meal (finely ground almonds)
1 tablesp. sugar
7 eggs
3 egg yolks
1 cup sugar
⅔ cup cake flour
1 teasp. grated orange rind

Mix almond meal, sugar, and 1 egg to a smooth paste. Combine remaining 6 eggs, 3 egg yolks, and 1 cup of sugar in saucepan, and cook over very low flame, beating constantly, until mixture is lukewarm. Remove from heat, and continue to beat until mixture is thick and fluffy, about 7 minutes. Add almond mixture. Add flour, 2 tablesp. at a time. Add orange rind and blend well. Pour batter into greased, 12-in. square pan lined with waxed paper, and bake at 375° 40 minutes. Serves 6 to 8.

ANGELA'S EASY WEDDING CAKE

TORTA DI NOZZE

This cake should be baked the day before the wedding. Assemble enough ingredients for 2 recipes, and have pans greased and lined with waxed paper before starting to bake.

BOTTOM TIER:

1 cup butter
2 cups sugar
4 eggs
1 cup milk
3 cups flour
4 teasp. baking powder
1 teasp. vanilla
1 teasp. almond or rose extract

Cream butter and sugar, and add eggs 1 at a time, beating well after each addition. Add milk and beat. Sift flour, measure, and resift with baking powder. Add to creamed mixture, add flavoring, and beat 2 minutes. Pour batter into 12-in. torte pan greased and lined with waxed paper. Bake in moderate oven 350° 60 minutes. Remove from oven and cool in pan 5 minutes. Turn cake out of pan, peel off waxed paper, and place on large round cake plate covered with a lace doily. Ice sides with butter frosting.

Make the batter again, following the same directions. Grease 3 round pans, one 10-in., one 8-in., and one 6-in., and line them with waxed paper. Fill each pan about two-thirds full of batter, and bake in moderate oven 350° 30 minutes.

Remove from oven, and proceed as with first tier. Frost the *sides* of each layer with butter frosting, and also the top of the last tier. Keep layers separate.

BUTTER FROSTING

½ cup butter	*Juice of 1 lemon*
4 cups sifted confectioners sugar	

Cream butter and sugar, gradually add lemon juice, until frosting is of spreading consistency. This amount will cover all layers.

On the day of the wedding, prepare filling and decorative frosting.

FILLING

2 pkgs. prepared vanilla pudding	*1 tablesp. rum*

Follow directions on pudding package. Add rum.

DECORATIVE FROSTING

8 cups sifted confectioners sugar	*6 egg whites, slightly beaten*
	Juice of 1 lemon

Sift sugar into a bowl. Make a well in sugar and put slightly beaten egg whites into it. Add lemon juice a little at a time, beating constantly until smooth. Add only enough juice to make frosting easy to beat. Beat with an electric mixer at low speed 10 minutes, until a spoon inserted into the frosting stands up straight without falling over. Cover the bowl with a damp cloth until you are ready to use the icing.

To put the cake together, spread vanilla filling on bottom tier. Set 10-in. tier in place, spread this with filling, then put on the 8-in. tier, spread with filling, and then the 6-in. tier on top. Frost the top of the 6-in. tier with frosting. Reserve a small amount of frosting, and use the rest to decorate the edges of each layer, using a cake decorator. Cut off the stems of 4 white roses or daisies, leaving about an inch. Dip the stems into the portion of reserved frosting, and insert the flowers in the corners of the cake. Set a miniature bride and groom in the center of the top tier.

ITALIAN YELLOW CAKE

TORTA GIALLO

6 egg yolks
1 cup sugar
Grated rind of 1 orange
¼ cup melted butter
1 cup sifted cake flour

Combine egg yolks, sugar, and grated orange rind in the top of a double boiler, and place over hot, not boiling, water. Beat mixture constantly until it is lukewarm. Remove from heat, add melted butter and sifted flour, and mix thoroughly until well blended. Pour into 2 greased 9-in. cake pans and dust with confectioners sugar. Bake in moderate oven 350° until cake shrinks from the side of pan, about 40 minutes. When done, take cake out of pans immediately and cool on rack. Serve plain; or, dust the tops of the cakes with confectioners sugar; or, sprinkle them with ⅓ cup rum or sherry. Serves 8 to 10.

Fillings

BRANDY CREAM WHIP

BRANDY FRUSTA

1 pt. heavy cream
2 tablesp. sugar
Pinch of unflavored gelatin
1 tablesp. brandy

Combine all ingredients in a chilled bowl and whip until stiff enough to hold shape. This is an excellent filling, frosting, or sauce. Makes 2½ cups.

CREAM FILLING #1

1 egg white
¼ cup confectioners sugar
½ cup heavy cream
1 teasp. almond extract

Beat egg whites until they will hold a peak. Add sugar gradually, continuing to beat until stiff but not dry. Whip cream until stiff, add almond extract, and fold whipped cream into egg whites. This type of filling may be used to fill St. Joseph's cream puffs, cannoli, cassata, tarts, or any layer cake.

CREAM FILLING #2

⅓ cup cornstarch
½ cup sugar
3 cups milk
3 egg yolks, slightly beaten
2 teasp. almond extract
2 tablesp. grated chocolate, unsweetened or semi-sweet

Combine cornstarch, sugar, and milk in a saucepan, add egg yolks, and blend well. Cook over low flame until mixture comes to boil. Remove from heat, add almond extract and chocolate. Mix thoroughly and cool before using.

FILBERT FILLING

AVELLANA LIMATURA

½ pt. heavy cream
1 tablesp. confectioners sugar
½ teasp. brandy, cognac, orange flower water, or sherry
¼ cup chopped filberts
3 tablesp. candied fruit, chopped fine

Whip cream until almost stiff; add sugar, and desired flavoring, and continue to whip to stiffness. Fold in nuts and candied fruit. This is an especially good filling for cream puffs or for layer cakes. Will fill a 9-in. 2 layer cake, or 12 puffs.

RICOTTA CAKE FILLING

LIMATURA DI RICOTTA

1 lb. fresh ricotta
3 tablesp. milk
¼ cup confectioners sugar
3 tablesp. rum, brandy, or maraschino

Combine all ingredients and beat until creamy. Store in refrigerator until ready to use. It will keep 3 days. This filling may be used for layer cakes, cream puffs, or as a dessert by itself.

RUM CREAM FILLING

CREMA AL RUM

3 cups milk
¼ cup cornstarch
1 cup sugar
3 eggs, beaten until foamy
3 oz. (3 sqs.) unsweetened chocolate
2 tablesp. rum; or 1 tablesp. rum extract

Combine milk, cornstarch, sugar, and beaten eggs in saucepan. Add chocolate, and cook over low flame until mixture boils. Then boil 2 minutes more, until it is thick. Stir constantly while heating. Remove from heat, cool, and add rum. VARIATION: Substitute 2 tablesp. strong coffee for rum.

Frostings

ALMOND FROSTING

GHIACCIATA DI MANDORLE

3 cups sifted confectioners sugar
2 egg whites
1½ teasp. almond extract
Pinch of salt
1 teasp. warm water

Beat egg whites with 2 cups sugar until fluffy. Add balance of sugar, flavoring, salt, and water, and beat well. This is enough frosting for the top and sides of a 9-in. 2 layer cake.

APRICOT FROSTING

GHIACCIATA DI ALBICOCCA

1 cup sifted confectioners sugar
4 tablesp. apricot jam
2 tablesp. brandy; or, 2 tablesp. any fruit juice

Combine all ingredients, and blend well. If necessary add a little more confectioners sugar so that frosting is of right consistency to spread. Enough to frost a 9 by 9 loaf cake, or fill a 9-in. layer cake.

CHOCOLATE FROSTING

GHIACCIATA DI CIOCCOLATA

¼ cup butter
3 oz. (3 sqs.) unsweetened chocolate
2 tablesp. confectioners sugar
1 teasp. rum or strong coffee; or, ½ teasp. vanilla extract

Mix ingredients in top of double boiler, and cook over hot, not boiling, water, stirring constantly, until chocolate melts. Do not allow to boil. This will frost an 8 by 8 loaf cake. It is a very thin frosting, but good.

CINNAMON FROSTING

GHIACCIATA ALLA CANNELLA

¼ cup butter
1 egg
1 teasp. cinnamon
1½ tablesp. cocoa
3 cups confectioners sugar
1½ tablesp. hot strong coffee

Cream butter, egg, and dry ingredients. Add coffee and continue beating until smooth. Enough to frost top and sides of a 9-in. 2 layer cake.

COFFEE FROSTING

GHIACCIATA AL CAFFE

½ cup butter
1 cup confectioners sugar
1 egg
3 tablesp. strong coffee
¼ cup cocoa
1 teasp. brandy, vanilla, rum, or other liqueur

Cream butter and sugar. Add egg, and beat well. Add remaining ingredients and beat until smooth. Enough frosting for the top and sides of a 9-in. 2 layer cake. The frosting may be garnished with chopped toasted almonds, if desired.

MERINGUE FROSTING

GHIACCIATA MIRINGHE

1¾ cups sugar
½ cup water
5 egg whites
½ teasp. vanilla
Food coloring (optional)

Combine sugar and water in saucepan, and cook over medium flame until syrup spins a long thread from the tip of spoon. Remove from heat and add vanilla. Set pan in cold water and while syrup is cooling beat egg whites until stiff but not dry. Add beaten egg whites to syrup and beat constantly until mixture becomes a smooth paste. Tint with 4 drops of coloring, if desired. This frosting may be used as decorative icing, or to make meringues, tarts, or pies.

PALERMO ICING

GHIACCIATA ALLA PALERMITANA

4 cups sifted confectioners sugar
½ cup butter
Grated rind of 1 lemon
½ teasp. lemon juice

Cream all ingredients until smooth. Add more lemon juice, if necessary, so frosting will be of good consistency to spread. Enough frosting for top and sides of 2 9-in. layers.

VARIATION: Orange rind and orange juice may be substituted for lemon.

RUM FROSTING

GHIACCIATA AL RUM

1 cup butter
4 cups sifted confectioners sugar
⅔ cup cocoa
2 egg yolks
2 tablesp. rum

Cream butter, cocoa, and sugar, until well blended. Beat egg yolks until thick and lemon colored, and add them to creamed mixture. Add rum, and beat thoroughly. Enough frosting for top and sides of 2 9-in. layers.

Sauces

BRANDY CHERRY SAUCE

SALSA DI CILIEGIE

½ cup sugar
¼ cup water
1 2-in. piece of stick cinnamon
1 tablesp. cornstarch
¾ cup cherry juice drained from canned cherries
1 cup canned pitted Bing cherries
1 tablesp. brandy

Combine sugar, water, and cinnamon stick in saucepan and boil over medium flame 5 minutes, stirring occasionally. Remove from heat and discard cinnamon stick. Mix together in another saucepan the cornstarch and cherry juice. Pour sugar syrup over cherry juice and blend well. Cook over medium flame until thick and clear, stirring constantly. Remove from heat, add cherries and brandy, and serve over plain cake or ice cream. Enough for 4 servings.

DESSERT SAUCE

SALSA DOLCE

½ cup sugar
3 tablesp. butter
1 egg, beaten
½ cup sherry

Cream butter and sugar until light, and beat in egg. Add sherry gradually, still beating, and cook in top of double boiler over hot, not boiling, water, for 3 minutes, beating constantly. Serve hot over puddings, ice cream, or plain cake. 4 servings.

FIG SAUCE

SALSA DI FICI

1 cup pulled figs
½ cup sugar
1 cup water
2 tablesp. grated lemon or orange rind
1 piece of stick cinnamon, 3 in. long
1 tablesp. brandy, rum, or sherry

Combine figs, water, sugar, lemon rind, and cinnamon stick, and cook over low heat until figs are tender, 20 minutes. Remove from flame, add brandy. Discard cinnamon stick. Serve figs hot as a dessert sauce over ice cream or cake. Serves 4.

LEMON SAUCE

SALSA DI LIMONE

2 cups sugar
Juice of ½ lemon
6 eggs, well beaten
¼ cup butter

Combine sugar, lemon juice, and well beaten eggs, and cook over hot water until thick, about 15 minutes. Stir frequently. Add butter and blend well. Remove from stove, and pour into sterilized jar and seal. Store in refrigerator until ready to use. May be used appropriately over any ice cream, pudding, or frozen dessert, or as a filling for cakes and tarts. Makes 1½ cups.

LIQUEUR SAUCE

SALSA DI LIQUORE

1 cup water
1 cup sugar
2 jiggers brandy, creme de menthe, creme de cacao, anisette, or rosolio

Boil water and sugar over low flame 10 minutes. Skim surface, cool, and add desired liqueur. Stir well. Store in refrigerator, and serve over ice cream, fresh fruit, or plain cake. Makes 1½ cups.

CHAPTER FOURTEEN

Cookies

IT IS SURPRISING TO FIND OUT IN WHAT LARGE QUANTITIES MOST Italian housewives bake *biscotti* (cookies) and *cucidata* (filled cookies). I have cut many of the following recipes in half, and the number of cookies each recipe makes is still very generous. I have indicated those cookies most often used for weddings and holidays, and have also included many baked for everyday eating in Italian homes.

BASIC ITALIAN COOKIES

BISCOTTI

5 cups flour
1 ½ cups sifted confectioners sugar
2 tablesp. baking powder
1 cup shortening
3 eggs
1 tablesp. vanilla

Sift flour and measure. Resift with sugar and baking powder on to a bread board or table top. Cut shortening into dry ingredients until mixture resembles coarse cornmeal. Make a well in flour and break eggs into it. Add vanilla, and knead dough well for about 5 minutes until it is smooth, adding a little more flour if dough seems too soft and sticky. Pinch off bits of dough about the size of an apricot, and form into desired shapes. Cookies may be baked as rings, strips, or in letters, such as the letter S. Place 1 in. apart on greased cookie sheet and bake in hot oven 450° 10 minutes, until golden brown. Watch carefully, because they burn easily. Makes 4 dozen.

EASY COOKIES

BISCOTTI FACILE

6 cups flour	*1 ½ cups shortening*
2 cups confectioners sugar	*5 eggs (reserve 1 egg white)*
1 ¾ tablesp. baking powder	*1 teasp. almond extract*

Sift flour, measure, and resift with sugar and baking powder. Cut shortening in with fingers until mixture resembles corn meal. Make a well in center of flour and put eggs and flavoring into it. Knead for 5 minutes. Pinch off pieces of dough the size of an apricot and roll between palms into strips the size and thickness of a finger. Beat reserved egg white slightly with a fork, and using a pastry brush, brush cookies with egg white. Place 1 in. apart on greased cookie sheet, and bake in moderate oven 350° 10 minutes until brown. Makes 6 dozen.

VARIATIONS: 1. Take a handful of dough, roll out an 18 in. rope ½ in. thick, and cut it into 2 in. pieces. Bake as directed.

2. Divide dough into 3 equal parts. Keep 1 part plain, and roll into desired shapes; add 1 cup chopped nuts to second part; roll third part into ropes, cut into 2 in. pieces, and roll pieces in ½ lb. sesame seeds. Bake as directed.

ALMOND BALLS

PASTINI DI MANDORLA

½ cup butter
1 cup sugar
1 egg
1 teasp. sherry; or, 1 teasp. lemon, orange, almond, or vanilla extract
2 cups sifted flour
1 teasp. baking powder
2 tablesp. milk
⅔ cup chopped almonds
¼ cup apricot jam or orange marmalade

Cream butter, sugar, eggs, and flavoring. Add flour, baking powder, and milk. Knead until well mixed. Pinch off small pieces of dough and roll between palms into balls. Roll balls in chopped almonds, and place on greased cookie sheets. With thumb make indentation in center of each cookie and fill with marmalade or apricot jam. Bake at 400° 12 to 15 minutes. 2 dozen.

ALMOND SLICES

BISCOTTI DI MANDORLA

½ cup sugar
1 cup butter or shortening
5 eggs
1 teasp. vanilla
4 cups sifted flour
2½ tablesp. baking powder
¼ teasp. salt
2½ cups chopped almonds

Cream butter and sugar. Add eggs one at a time, beating well after each addition. Add vanilla. Sift flour, measure, and resift with baking powder and salt. Add to creamed mixture. Add nuts. Transfer dough to lightly floured bread board and knead well for 5 minutes, adding a little more flour if dough seems too soft and sticky. Roll dough into a 5 in. square loaf about ¾ in. thick. Brush top of loaf with milk, and then cut it into 1 in. slices. Place slices on greased cookie sheet 2 in. apart, and bake in moderate oven 350° until light brown, 12 to 15 minutes. Makes 28 to 30 slices.

MAMA MIA ANISE BREAD

PANE ANICE DI MAMA MIA

1 cup shortening or butter
½ cup sugar
6 eggs
4 drops anise oil
1 tablesp. anise seeds
3 teasp. baking powder
Pinch of salt
5 cups flour

Cream butter, sugar, and eggs. Add anise oil and anise seed, and stir with a wooden spoon until well blended. Sift flour, measure, and resift with baking powder and salt. Add dry ingredients to creamed mixture and knead 5 minutes, adding more flour a tablespoon at a time if dough is too sticky. Dough should be smooth and fairly soft. Roll dough out on lightly floured board into oblong loaf 4 by 9 in. Place loaf on greased cookie sheet and bake in moderate oven 350° 20 minutes, until light brown. Remove loaf from oven and cool slightly. Remove from cookie sheet, and cut loaf into 1 in. slices. Replace slices on cookie sheet, cut side down, and toast in hot oven 425° 3 or 4 minutes, until lightly brown on cut portion. Watch carefully during toasting to make sure that cookies do not burn. The toasting may be omitted, if desired, and the untoasted slices dipped in icing instead. These cookies keep well, especially when iced. Makes 2 dozen slices.

ICING

2 cups granulated sugar
1 cup water
2 teasp. anise flavor

Mix ingredients in saucepan and cook over medium flame until syrup forms a soft ball in cold water, about 10 minutes. This thin icing may be used on all cookies that call for frosting.

VARIATION: Add 2 cups coarsely chopped almonds to dough with flour. Bake as directed.

JOE'S APRICOT COOKIES

PASTINI DI ALBICOCCA

2 cups flour
½ teasp. salt
2 teasp. baking powder
1 cup butter
1 cup sugar
¼ cup apricot jam
2 eggs
¼ cup light cream

Sift flour, measure, and resift with salt and baking powder. Cream butter and sugar, add jam and eggs, and beat well. Gradually add sifted dry ingredients, and blend well. Drop by rounded tablesp. on an ungreased cookie sheet 2 in. apart. Bake in 375° oven until light brown, 12 to 15 minutes. 4½ dozen.

CHOCOLATE MACAROONS

AMARETTI CIOCCOLATI

2 oz. (2 sqs.) unsweetened chocolate
3 egg whites
2¼ cups confectioners sugar
1 tablesp. cold water
1 teasp. rum, or any desired flavoring
2½ cups finely ground almonds
Candied cherries or blanched almonds

Melt chocolate over hot water. Beat egg whites until they hold a peak, and gradually beat in sugar. Combine melted chocolate, water, and rum, and fold into egg whites. Fold in almond meal gently. Drop by teaspoonfuls on a greased cookie sheet lined with waxed paper, and bake in moderate oven 350° 15 minutes. As the macaroons come out of oven place a candied cherry or almond in center of each. Let cool on sheet for 1 minute and then remove gently with spatula.

Store in airtight container for 24 hours before using. They will keep well. Makes 5 dozen.

CHOCOLATE ALMOND BALLS

DADRIO

5 cups sifted flour
2½ cups confectioners sugar
2 tablesp. baking powder
¼ cup cocoa
2 cups coarsely chopped almonds
½ cup shortening
2 eggs, slightly beaten
1 6-oz. can evaporated milk

Sift flour, measure, and resift with sugar, baking powder, and cocoa. Add nuts, and mix well. Cut shortening into dry ingredients with fingers until mixture resembles coarse corn meal. Make a well in center of flour and put eggs and milk into it. Knead dough until smooth, about 5 minutes. If it seems too dry, add water 1 teaspoon at a time until mixture holds together. Pinch off pieces of dough the size of a walnut, and roll into balls between the palms of hands. Place balls on greased cookie sheet 1 in. apart, and bake in moderate oven 350° 18 to 20 minutes, until toothpick inserted in center of ball comes out clean. Watch carefully, as these burn easily. Frost as soon as they come out of oven with any desired frosting. Makes 6 dozen. Caution: Handle these cookies very carefully, as they are quite delicate and will crumble.

CHOCOLATE PEANUT COOKIES

BISCOTTI DI CIOCCOLATA CON ARACHIDE

8 cups sifted flour
⅔ cup cocoa
1⅓ cups sugar
1 tablesp. baking powder
2 cups shortening
3 eggs
2 teasp. vanilla
¾ cup milk
1½ cups shelled unsalted peanuts, coarsely chopped
1 tablesp. oil

Sift flour, measure, and resift with cocoa, sugar, and baking powder. Cut shortening into dry ingredients with fingers until mixture resembles corn meal. Make a well in center of flour and break eggs into it. Add flavoring, milk, and chopped peanuts. Knead dough until smooth, about 5 minutes. Brush surface of dough with oil, and knead 1 minute longer. Break off pieces of dough the size of a walnut and shape them into balls between the palms of the hands. Place balls on greased cookie sheet 1 in. apart, and bake in moderate oven 350° 20 minutes, until toothpick inserted in center of ball comes out clean. Remove from sheet and cool on rack. If desired these cookies may be frosted with any thin confectioners frosting. Makes 8 dozen cookies.

CHRISTMAS COOKIES

PASTINI DI NATALE

2½ cups sifted flour
Pinch of salt
1 tablesp. baking powder
1 cup sugar
¼ cup shortening
1 egg yolk, slightly beaten
1 teasp. grated orange or lemon rind; or, 1 teasp. almond extract
½ cup milk
1 egg white
1⅔ cups confectioners sugar
½ cup candied cherries
½ cup candied chopped fruit
½ cup chopped pistachios or almonds

Sift flour, measure, and resift with salt, baking powder, and sugar. Cut in shortening with fingers until mixture resembles corn meal. Make a well in flour and put in the milk, slightly beaten egg yolk, and flavoring. Knead into smooth ball, about 5 minutes. Set in refrigerator for 15 minutes. Roll dough out on lightly floured board to ¼ in. thick, and cut into any desired shapes. Place on ungreased cookie sheet. Brush tops with egg white which has been beaten until foamy with confectioners sugar. Decorate tops with bits of cherries, fruit, and nuts. Bake in moderate oven 375° until golden brown, about 10 minutes. Cool cookies on rack, and if desired, dust with powdered sugar. Store in cool dry place. Makes 5 dozen.

CHRISTMAS FILLED COOKIES

CUCIDATA

FILLING:

½ lb. pulled figs
½ lb. seedless raisins
1 strip orange or tangerine peel 2 in. long
¼ lb. sweet chocolate
¼ cup honey
Pinch of pepper
¼ teasp. cinnamon
¼ teasp. ground allspice
¼ lb. chopped candied fruit

Put figs, raisins, orange peel, and chocolate through food chopper, using medium blade. If ingredients stick in the grinder, add 1 tablesp. cold water. Add honey, spices, and fruit to mixture, and blend well.

COOKIE DOUGH

8 cups sifted flour
1 cup sugar
3 tablesp. baking powder
¼ teasp. salt
1½ cups shortening
3 eggs
1 cup milk, approximately
1½ teasp. vanilla extract
1½ teasp. anise flavoring

Sift flour, measure, and resift with sugar, baking powder, and salt. Cut in shortening with fingers until mixture resembles corn meal. Make a well in flour, and break eggs into it. Add half of milk, and both flavorings. Knead well for 5 minutes, adding the balance of the milk gradually as you knead. Add only enough milk to make a medium soft dough which is easy to handle. Divide dough into 3 parts. Roll each portion of the dough into circular sheets 1/8 in. thick, and cut into various shapes. Cut two shapes for each cookie. Place 1 rounded tablesp. of filling on one cookie, then cover with another cookie. Make a 1/4 in. slit in the top cookie with a sharp knife; moisten the edges of the bottom cookie with cold water, and press the 2 together with the tines of a fork. Make 1/8 in. slits all around the edges about 1/4 in. apart. Bake on greased cookie sheet in moderate oven 375° until light brown, 18 to 25 minutes. Remove from oven and frost while hot. Makes 10 dozen cookies.

FROSTING

3 cups confectioners sugar
3 tablesp. melted butter
1 tablesp. vanilla
1/4 cup barely lukewarm milk

Combine all ingredients and blend well. Add a little more milk if necessary. Frost cookies, and then sprinkle with colored sprinkles.

COCOA BALLS

POLPETTE DI CIOCCOLATA

2 cups chocolate wafer crumbs; or 2 cups lady finger crumbs
1/4 cup cocoa
2 cups confectioners sugar
1 cup finely ground almonds or pecans
1 cup chopped almonds or pecans
1/2 cup rum, whiskey, or sherry
3 tablesp. corn syrup

Combine crumbs, cocoa, confectioners sugar, ground nuts, and chopped nuts. Mix with hands until well blended. Combine rum and syrup and pour into dry ingredients. Pinch off a heaping teasp. and roll into a ball the size of a walnut. You must work quickly, or the mixture will get too dry to roll.

Place 1½ cups confectioners sugar in a bowl. Roll balls in sugar and place in tightly covered container. Store in refrigerator 2 days before using. These cookies will keep indefinitely. Makes 4 dozen.

CORN MEAL COOKIES

PASTINI DI POLENTA

1 cup yellow corn meal
1 cup sifted flour
¼ cup confectioners sugar
3 teasp. baking powder
Grated rind of 1 lemon
1 cup coarsely chopped nuts
1 cup shortening
2 eggs, slightly beaten
1 tablesp. orange juice
⅛ lb. glacé cherries

Combine dry ingredients, lemon rind, and nuts. Cut shortening in with fingers until mixture resembles small peas. Make a well in center of dry ingredients, and pour slightly beaten eggs and orange juice into it. Knead well for 5 minutes until smooth. Chill in refrigerator ½ hour. Then roll out on lightly floured bread board or table top until ½ in. thick. Cut in fancy shapes with cookie cutter, and make an indentation in the center of each cookie with thumb. Place a glacé cherry on top of cookie, and bake on a greased cookie sheet in hot oven 425° until golden brown, 10 minutes. Frost if desired. Makes 3 dozen. Delicious with any kind of wine.

PHILOMENA'S FILBERT ROLLS

DOLCE DI NOCE

1 cup butter
1¼ cups confectioners sugar
3 eggs
2 teasp. vanilla or anise flavor
4 cups sifted flour
1 lb. toasted chopped filberts

Cream butter and sugar and add eggs one at a time, beating well after each addition. Add flavoring and blend well. Add sifted flour and nuts, and knead gently. Dough should be soft and sticky. Pinch off pieces of dough the size of walnuts, and form into small rolls the thickness of a finger. Place on a greased cookie sheet 1 in. apart, and bake in a moderate oven 350° until lightly browned, 12 to 15 minutes. Makes 4 to 5 dozen cookies.

FLORENTINE SWEETS

DOLCE ALLA FIORENTINO

¼ lb. blanched almonds — *½ cup sugar*
¼ lb. candied orange peel — *1 tablesp. grated lemon rind*
1 tablesp. flour — *½ cup milk*
2 oz. sweet chocolate

Put nuts and candied orange peel through a food chopper, using medium blade. Combine ground mixture with flour, sugar, lemon rind, and milk. Mix until well blended. Take heaping tablespoonfuls of the mixture and place them on a greased cookie sheet 1 in. apart. Flatten these into 2 in. rounds with the back of a spoon or the bottom of a glass. Bake in a moderate oven 350° about 15 minutes, and cool on cake rack. Melt chocolate over hot water in top of double boiler. Dip the bottom of each cookie in melted chocolate, and let dry upside down on a plate. Chill before serving. Makes 1 dozen.

GODMOTHER'S BISCOTTI

BISCOTTI MADRINA

5¾ cups sifted flour — *¾ cup shortening*
1 tablesp. baking powder — *4 eggs*
1¼ cups sugar — *½ teasp. vanilla*
Juice of ½ orange

Sift flour, measure, and resift with baking powder and sugar into a bowl or on to a bread board or table top. Cut shortening into dry ingredients until it resembles coarse corn meal. Make a well in flour. Beat eggs, vanilla and orange juice with a fork until well blended. Pour this mixture into the well in the flour, and knead for 5 minutes until smooth. Pinch off pieces of dough and mold into rolls the size and thickness of a finger. Bake in moderate oven 325° 6 to 10 minutes. Makes 4 dozen.

VARIATION: Two Tone Cookies.

Divide cookie dough into two parts. Add 6 drops of green vegetable coloring to one half of dough, and 6 drops of pink vegetable coloring to the other half, kneading until well blended. Pinch off piece of pink dough the size of an egg, and roll this until it is 12 in. long and the thickness of a finger. Repeat with a piece of green dough. Place these two rolls close together on a cookie sheet. Repeat rolls until all of the dough has been used. Place the double rolls 2 in. apart on the cookie sheet, as they will rise as they bake. Bake in moderate oven 325° 6 to 10 minutes. Remove from oven, cool, and frost immediately, garnishing with chopped nuts or coconut if desired. Use fingers to spread frosting. As soon as rolls are frosted, cut them into 1 in. slices.

FROSTING

Combine ½ lb. confectioners sugar with 2 tablesp. boiling water. Mix until smooth, and spread at once. If frosting gets too thick, add a few drops of boiling water.

HAZELNUT DELIGHTS

NOCCIOLLETTE

1 cup butter
¼ cup confectioners sugar
3 tablesp. honey
1 tablesp. sherry, whiskey, brandy, or rum
1¼ cups chopped hazelnuts
2 cups sifted flour

Cream butter, sugar, and honey. Add wine, and blend well. Add nuts and flour and knead dough until smooth. Pinch off pieces of dough the size of a walnut, and roll into balls. Place on a greased cookie sheet 1 in. apart, and bake in a moderate oven 350° until light brown, about 15 minutes. Remove from oven, and cool slightly. Roll in confectioners sugar while still hot. Makes 2½ dozen.

HONEY SLICES

MIELE BISCOTTI

3 cups sifted flour
3 teasp. baking powder
½ cup sugar
½ teasp. ground cinnamon
½ cup chopped almonds, filberts, or walnuts
½ cup shortening
3 eggs (reserve 1 egg white)
½ cup honey

Sift flour, measure, and resift with baking powder, sugar, and cinnamon. Add nuts. Cut shortening in with fingers until well blended. Warm honey slightly. Make a well in flour, put eggs and warm honey into it, and knead into a smooth ball. Dough should be firm and manageable; if it is too soft and sticky, add more flour. Roll dough into oblong loaf 5 in. wide and ½ in. thick. Place on a greased cookie sheet, brush top with reserved egg white, and bake in moderate oven 350° until golden brown, about 30 minutes. Remove from oven, cool slightly, and cut into 1 in. slices. Store these slices in an airtight container, and they will keep fresh for weeks. The longer they keep, the better their flavor will be. Makes about 20 slices.

ST. JOSEPH'S CREAM PUFFS

SFINGE DI SAN GIUSEPPE

1 cup hot water
½ cup butter
1 cup sifted flour
4 eggs
½ teasp. grated lemon rind
½ teasp. grated orange rind
24 candied or maraschino cherries

Boil water and butter in a saucepan, add sifted flour, and stir constantly until smooth. Cook over medium flame until mixture leaves sides of pan clean, about 2 minutes, stirring constantly. Remove from heat and allow to cool slightly. Add eggs 1 at a time, beating well after each addition. Add grated rind and blend. Drop by tablespoons on ungreased cookie sheet 2 in. apart and bake in moderate oven 350° until puffs are light, about 30 minutes. Remove from oven, and cut opening in the middle of top. Cool thoroughly and fill with one of the following fillings:

FILLING #1

2 eggs, slightly beaten
3 tablesp. sugar
1 tablesp. corn starch
1 cup milk
½ teasp. almond extract

Mix all ingredients except almond extract in saucepan and cook over low flame 10 minutes, until thick. Stir constantly. Cool slightly, add flavoring, and fill puffs.

FILLING #2

1 lb. ricotta
1 tablesp. honey
1 tablesp. grated orange rind
2 tablesp. grated sweet chocolate

Mash ricotta and honey, add orange rind and chocolate, and blend until creamy. Fill puffs.

Store filled puffs in refrigerator until ready to serve. Makes 24 puffs.

LADY FINGERS

SAVOIARDI

3 eggs, separated
½ teasp. almond extract
¼ teasp. salt
⅓ cup sugar
½ cup sifted cake flour
1 teasp. baking powder

Beat egg yolks until thick and lemon colored. Beat in almond extract. Beat egg whites until stiff but not dry, and gradually beat in sugar until whites are glossy and very stiff. Fold egg yolks gently into whites. Fold in sifted dry ingredients. Drop batter by tablespoons on ungreased cookie sheet forming fingers 3 in. long and 1 in. wide. Bake in moderate oven 350° 10 minutes, until light brown. Remove immediately from cookie sheet and cool on rack. Makes 3 dozen.

NEAPOLITAN TARTLETS

TARTINI NAPOLETANI

2 cups sifted flour
2 tablesp. confectioners sugar
1 cup butter, chilled
½ cup cold water

Sift flour and sugar together into a bowl. Make a well in center, and put butter and water into it. Knead until dough is smooth and soft, about 5 minutes. Roll in waxed paper and put in refrigerator.

While dough is chilling, prepare filling:

½ cup sugar
¼ cup flour
1 egg slightly beaten
1¼ cups milk
1 teasp. orange extract
1 cup finely ground almonds
2 egg yolks, slightly beaten

Combine sugar, flour, egg, and milk in saucepan, and stir until well blended. Cook over low heat until thick and creamy, about 10 minutes, stirring constantly. Remove from flame, add orange flavoring and ground almonds and mix well. Cool thoroughly.

Roll chilled dough out to ¼ in. thickness and cut into 2½ in. squares. Fill the center of each square with 1 level tablesp. of filling. Fold 2 opposite ends of the squares in to the center, like a turnover, and press together with thumb, gently. Brush top of tartlet with slightly beaten egg yolk, and bake on a lightly greased cookie sheet in moderate oven 375° 30 minutes. Cool on cake rack and dust with confectioners sugar. Makes 18 tartlets.

SUGAR BALLS

PASTINI DI ZUCCHERO

¾ cup butter
1 cup sugar
1 egg
1 teasp. almond extract
1 teasp. baking powder
2 cups sifted flour
½ cup sugar
½ teasp. ground cinnamon

Cream butter, sugar, egg, and almond extract. Add baking powder and flour and knead 1 minute. Mix together ½ cup sugar and cinnamon. Pinch off pieces of dough about the size of a walnut, and roll into balls with palms of hands. Dip in sugar and cinnamon, and place on a greased cookie sheet 2 in. apart. Bake at 400° until light brown, about 10 minutes. Makes 3 dozen.

WEDDING BREAD

PAN DI SPOSALIZIO

12 eggs, separated
10 drops anise oil
¾ cup confectioners sugar
¾ cup sifted pastry flour
1 tablesp. anise seeds, whole or crushed

All ingredients must be at room temperature. Beat egg yolks, adding one at a time, until thick and lemon colored. Add anise oil, and gradually blend in powdered sugar. Combine flour and anise seeds, and beat gradually into egg yolks. Beat egg whites until foamy, and fold into yolks. Grease three 6 by 8 in. loaf pans and pour about 2 in. of batter into each pan. Sprinkle tops with confectioners sugar and bake in moderate oven 350° 25 to 30 minutes until delicately browned. Cool and slice crosswise into 1 in. slices. If desired, the slices may be toasted on a greased cookie sheet in a slow oven for 10 minutes. These cookies are excellent with coffee or wine. It is customary to serve them at wedding breakfasts. Makes 2 dozen.

CHAPTER FIFTEEN

Pies and Pastry

PASTRY CRUST

SFOGLIATA

1½ cups sifted flour
1 teasp. salt
¼ cup butter
½ cup shortening
2 tablesp. sherry

Chill all ingredients 30 minutes before using. Also chill pie pan and rolling pin. Put flour, butter, salt, and shortening in a bowl, and cut shortening into flour with a pastry blender or fork until particles are the size of split peas. Add only enough sherry to make ingredients stick together. Wrap pastry in waxed paper and chill in refrigerator 30 minutes.

Divide dough into 2 parts. Roll bottom crust a little larger than top, if making a two-crust pie. Roll out on a lightly floured board from the center toward the edges. Place the crust in chilled pie pan, and press flat with fingers. Prick bottom and sides well with a fork. Flute edges. Place shell in refrigerator until ready to bake. Preheat oven to 450°, and bake shell for 10 minutes, until brown. Cool. Fill with any desired filling. This makes 2 9-in. pastry shells, 1 9-in. double crust pie, or 16 tart shells.

PHILOMENA'S PASTRY

PASTA FROLLA

2 cups sifted cake flour
½ teasp. salt
¼ cup sugar
½ cup butter, room temperature
3 egg yolks
1 teasp. grated lemon rind

Sift flour, measure, and resift with salt and sugar. Make a well in center of flour and put butter and eggs into it. Knead thoroughly 1 minute. Shape into a ball, wrap in waxed paper, and chill 1 hour or longer. Roll on lightly floured board to fit pie pan, and bake in preheated hot 450° oven 15 minutes; then reduce heat to 300° and bake 2 minutes longer. Fill shell with any desired filling. Makes 2 9-in. shells, 1 9-in. double crust pie, or 16 tart shells. Excellent for all fine pastries and tarts.

PINE NUT PIE

TORTA DI PIGNOLI

CRUST:

2 cups flour
1 teasp. salt
2 tablesp. sugar
2 egg yolks, slightly beaten
1 teasp. grated lemon or orange rind
½ cup butter
¼ cup white wine or water

Sift flour, measure, and resift with salt and sugar. Add egg yolk, grated rind and butter. Mix lightly with fingers until mixture resembles corn meal. Sprinkle wine or water over dry ingredients ½ teasp. at a time, using only enough liquid in all to hold mixture together. Roll dough out on lightly floured board, and place it in a *greased* 9-in. pie plate. Pour filling in crust. Roll scraps of dough out again and cut into ½ to 1 in. strips with pastry fluter or knife. Arrange strips 1 in. apart on top of filling, trimming off uneven ends, and bringing them out to meet crust. Bake in moderate oven 375° 30 minutes, until filling is firm. Serves 6.

FILLING:

2½ cups milk
3 tablesp. sugar
1 tablesp. butter
Pinch of salt
½ cup semolina (Cream of Wheat)
2 eggs, well beaten
Pinch of nutmeg or cinnamon
½ cup chopped pine nuts

Combine milk, sugar, butter, and salt, and cook over low heat. When milk comes to a boil, add semolina gradually, stirring constantly to prevent lumping, and continue to cook over low fire 10 minutes. Cool slightly, add beaten eggs and nutmeg, and beat with rotary beater until smooth. Add nuts and blend well. Pour into unbaked pie shell, and bake as directed.

NOTE: Pistachios or almonds may be substituted for pine nuts. Pine nuts are difficult to shell, so when you buy them, be sure you get them already shelled.

RICOTTA PIE

TORTA DI RICOTTA

2 unbaked 9-in. pastry shells, see p. 225
1½ lbs. ricotta
¼ cup flour
2 tablesp. lemon juice
3 eggs, separated
½ pt. heavy cream

Rub ricotta through a fine sieve. Add sugar and blend in flour and lemon juice. Beat thoroughly. Beat egg yolks until thick and lemon colored, and fold them into ricotta. Beat cream until stiff; fold into ricotta. Beat egg whites until stiff and fold into ricotta. Pour filling into unbaked pastry shells, and bake in slow oven 300° 1 hour. Pie will be just set. Turn off oven heat, and leave the pies in the oven without opening the door for 1 hour. Then remove from oven and cool thoroughly. Dust tops with powdered sugar. Serves 12.

NOTE: 2 tablesp. of orange flower water, sherry, cherry liqueur, or rum may be used instead of lemon juice. Or, 1 teasp. of almond extract may be used.

Fried Pastry

FRIED BOWKNOTS

CENCI

3 cups sifted flour
Pinch of salt
2 tablesp. confectioners sugar
2 eggs, slightly beaten
4 egg yolks, slightly beaten
1 tablesp. rum, brandy, or any white wine
2 cups peanut or salad oil

Sift flour, measure, and resift with salt and sugar. Make a well in center of dry ingredients, and put eggs, egg yolks, and rum into it. Knead thoroughly 10 minutes, until smooth. Add more flour if dough is too soft—this should be a very firm dough. Cover dough with a towel and let stand 1 hour. Divide dough into 4 parts. Roll one part at a time out on a lightly floured board to paper thinness. Cut into strips ½ in. wide and 6 in. long. Tie each strip into a loose bowknot or twist. Place on a cloth and let dry for about 5 minutes. Then fry bowknots in hot 375° oil until lightly brown, turning once. Lift out of oil carefully with slotted spoon and drain on unglazed paper. Place drained bowknots on large plate and sprinkle with powdered sugar. Serves 8 to 12.

CANNOLI

Cannoli are delicious hollow cylinders of fried pastry dough which are stuffed with sweet fillings and served as desserts. The dough is rolled paper thin, and then molded around a stick. (An unpainted, well-scrubbed broom handle cut into 6 inch pieces will furnish excellent sticks to use in making cannoli.) The edges of the dough are sealed with slightly beaten egg yolk, and then the shells are fried, stick and all. After the cannoli have been taken from the fat, the sticks are pushed out and the space is filled with whatever cream or ricotta filling you prefer.

HINTS FOR MAKING CANNOLI

1. Dough must be very stiff, and well kneaded.
2. Dough must be rolled to paper thinness with a rolling pin. This is very important. If the dough is not rolled thin enough, it will not blister, and good cannoli should have a blistered surface.
3. Fat should be 4 in. deep and very hot—390°.
4. Cannoli should be fried 2 at a time. Turn them once, and lift them out gently with a slotted spoon or tongs.
5. Push sticks out of cannoli very gently, being careful not to break shells. If the cannoli are hot, hold them with a cloth in the center, and push the stick out with a butter knife or the back of a spoon.
6. Fill shells with a butter knife, first from one end, and then from the other. Dip the ends of the filling in chopped nuts, and sprinkle cannoli with confectioners sugar.

EASY CANNOLI CRUST

4 cups sifted flour
1 tablesp. sugar
¼ teasp. cinnamon
¾ cup Italian red wine
1 egg yolk, slightly beaten

Sift flour, sugar and cinnamon together on to a bread board or table top. Make a well in dry ingredients, and pour wine into it. Knead dough until smooth and stiff, about 15 minutes. If dough seems moist and sticky, add flour. If it is too dry, add more wine. Cover dough and let stand two hours in a cool place. Then roll to paper thinness on lightly floured board. Cut into 5 inch circles, and wrap each circle around a stick which is about 6 inches long and 1 inch in diameter. Fold dough around stick loosely, so that ¼ inch of the stick protrudes at either end. Seal dough by brushing with egg yolk, and fry 2 cannoli at a time in deep hot fat for one minute, or until brown on both sides. Lift out gently with a slotted spoon or tongs, drain on unglazed paper, and cool. Remove sticks gently. Fill cannoli with one of the following fillings. Makes 2 dozen.

NOTE: The unfilled fried shells will keep for about 6 weeks in a cool dry place. The uncooked dough will keep in a refrigerator for two or three days. Filled cannoli should be served immediately. Keep filling in the refrigerator until you can serve cannoli, and fill just before serving.

BLUE RIBBON FILLING

3 lbs. ricotta
1 ¾ cups sifted confectioners sugar
½ teasp. cinnamon
2 tablesp. chopped citron
¼ cup semi-sweet chocolate bits

Beat ricotta in a large bowl for one minute. Add sugar, and beat until very light and creamy, about 5 minutes. Add cinnamon, citron, and chocolate, and mix until thoroughly blended. Keep this filling in refrigerator until ready to use. It may be prepared a day ahead of time. Makes enough to fill 25 cannoli.

MRS. BONGIORNO'S FILLING

1 cup sugar
1 cup water
2 lbs. ricotta
1 tablesp. candied orange peel, chopped
10 candied cherries, chopped
½ cup grated sweet chocolate; or, ½ cup semi-sweet chocolate bits
2 teasp. cinnamon
½ cup chopped pistachio nuts
½ cup confectioners sugar

Boil water and sugar in a saucepan for 10 minutes. Skim surface, and cool to room temperature.

Beat ricotta until creamy, about 3 minutes. Add cooled syrup, and beat about 2 minutes. Add chopped orange peel, chopped cherries, chocolate, and cinnamon, and stir until well blended. Fill cannoli, and dip ends of filling in pistachio nuts. Sprinkle with powdered sugar, and serve immediately. Filling will keep for three days in refrigerator. Makes enough for 25 cannoli.

CARNIVAL PUFFS

CARNEVALE SFINGE

1½ cups flour
Pinch of salt
3 teasp. baking powder
2 eggs
¼ cup sugar
½ cup water
2 cups salad or peanut oil
1 cup granulated sugar

Sift flour, salt, baking powder, and ¼ cup sugar together. Combine eggs and water, and blend into dry ingredients. Dip a tablespoon into a glass of cold water. Take 1 heaping tablesp. of batter, and, using a rubber scraper, slide it off spoon into hot oil. Fry 2 or 3 puffs at a time until golden brown, about 3 minutes. Drain on absorbent paper, and roll in sugar while still hot. Makes 10 or 12 puffs.

DOUGHNUTS

SFINGE

4 eggs
1 cup water
2 tablesp. sugar
2 cups sifted flour
2 teasp. baking powder
1 teasp. salt
2 cups salad oil
¾ cup sugar

Beat eggs and water together, until well blended. Sift dry ingredients together and stir into eggs. Cover, and set in warm place for 30 minutes. Heat oil to 350° and drop 1 tablesp. of batter at a time into the oil, cooking 3 doughnuts at a time. Drain on unglazed paper, and roll in sugar. Serve hot or cold. Makes 24 to 30 doughnuts.

FRIED RICOTTA

RICOTTA FRITTA

½ lb. ricotta
1 egg
2 tablesp. flour
1 tablesp. brandy, rum, or marsala
1 cup salad or peanut oil

Beat ricotta, egg, sugar, flour, and brandy in a bowl until creamy. Set in refrigerator for 3 hours. If batter is firm enough, shape into balls; if not, drop by teaspoonfuls into hot oil and fry until golden brown. Remove from oil with slotted spoon and serve immediately, either as a side dish or dessert. If used for dessert, roll the fried balls in confectioners sugar. Serves 6.

FRUIT FRITTERS: *See p. 255.*

HONEY CLUSTERS

STRUFOLI

2 cups sifted flour
3 eggs
Pinch of salt
2 cups salad oil
1¼ cups honey
½ cup sugar
3 tablesp. pine nuts (optional)
2 teasp. confectioners sugar

Sift flour. Make a well in center, and break eggs into it. Add salt, and knead until smooth. Roll dough out on lightly floured board until ¼ in. thick. Cut into ½ in. strips, and cut strips into tiny pieces ½ in. long. With the palm of the hands, shape these tiny pieces into balls the size of a filbert. Heat oil to 350° and drop balls in 3 at a time. Fry until lightly browned, turning them constantly with a wooden spoon. Remove balls and drain them in a colander.

Combine honey and sugar in saucepan and boil over low flame about 2 minutes, stirring constantly. Add fried dough 1 cup at a time, and cook in honey syrup, stirring constantly, for 1 minute. Remove and put strufoli on flat plate to cool. Sprinkle with pine nuts and powdered sugar as soon as they are cool enough to handle, and mold about 5 together in a cluster. Enough for 8. Strufoli will stay fresh for weeks if they are kept in a cool place.

NEAPOLITAN DOUGHNUTS

SFINGE DI NAPOLETANO

1 cup water
Pinch of salt
2 teasp. butter
2 teasp. sugar
1 jigger maraschino liqueur, or rum
1 cup sifted flour
2 cups salad oil

Combine water, salt, butter, sugar, and maraschino in a saucepan and stir in flour a little at a time. Cook over low heat

15 minutes, stirring constantly. Remove from stove and let cool to room temperature. Knead dough until smooth and then roll it out ¼ in. thick. Cut dough in rounds with doughnut cutter. Or, roll dough into strips the size of a finger, bring ends together, and seal. Prick the top of each doughnut with a fork, and fry in hot oil 350° until golden brown and crisp, about 3 minutes. Fry only 3 at a time, or the temperature of the oil will drop too much. Drain on unglazed paper and sprinkle with confectioners sugar. Makes 1 dozen doughnuts.

SWEET RAVIOLI

2 eggs
2 tablesp. butter
½ teasp. salt
3 tablesp. lukewarm water
¼ lb. ricotta
2⅛ cups flour
1 egg white
2 egg yolks
¼ teasp. cinnamon
2 tablesp. confectioners sugar
½ teasp. almond extract

Combine 2 eggs, butter, flour, salt, and water, and knead 1 minute until dough is smooth and stiff. Let stand 5 minutes.

Beat ricotta, egg white, egg yolks, cinnamon and sugar together until creamy. Divide dough in 2 parts. Roll into paper-thin sheets and cut 2 rounds for each ravioli. Place 1 teasp. ricotta filling in center of 1 round, cover with a second round, and press edges together firmly with a fork. Fry in hot oil 370° until golden brown, about 3 minutes. Remove from oil with slotted spoon and drain on unglazed paper. Sprinkle with confectioners sugar and serve immediately. Serves 4.

ST. LUCY'S SWEETS

DOLCI DI SANTA LUCIA

2 eggs
¼ teasp. salt
1 teasp. cinnamon
2 cups chestnut flour
2 cups peanut oil
2 tablesp. confectioners sugar

Beat eggs until thick and lemon colored. Mix salt, cinnamon, and flour, and sift into eggs. Knead well into smooth dough, adding more flour if necessary. Dough must be very stiff. Divide dough into 3 parts, and roll each out to ¼ in. thick. Cut into strips 1 in. wide and 4 in. long. Fry in hot oil 350° until golden brown. They will curl as they fry. Remove gently from hot oil with slotted spoon. Be careful, or they will break. Place on a platter and sprinkle with confectioners sugar. Enough for 10 people.

NOTE: Chestnut flour can be purchased in an Italian grocery store. White flour can be used to make these sweets on other days, but not on St. Lucy's day, since it is customary not to eat anything made with flour that day.

WINE STRIPS

STRISCIA DI VINO

2 cups flour
½ teasp. baking powder
3 tablesp. sugar
¼ cup butter
½ cup Italian red wine
2 cups oil
½ cup confectioners sugar
1 teasp. ground cinnamon

Sift flour, measure, and resift with baking powder and sugar. Cut butter into flour with fingers until mixture resembles corn meal. Make a well in flour and pour wine into it. Knead dough until smooth, about 5 minutes. Wrap in waxed paper and set aside for 2 hours, but do not chill. Heat oil in deep pan. Roll dough ¼ in. thick, and cut into strips 1 in. wide and 4 in. long. Drop about 4 at a time into hot oil, and fry until golden brown. Turn as they rise to surface. Remove from oil with slotted spoon and drain on absorbent paper. Combine confectioners sugar and cinnamon, and sprinkle over strips when they are cool. Makes 2½ dozen.

CHAPTER SIXTEEN

Puddings and Frozen Desserts

ALMOND CREAM

CREMA DI MANDORLA

1 envelope unflavored gelatin
3 tablesp. water
¼ cup chopped toasted almonds
2 tablesp. confectioners sugar
1 teasp. almond extract
½ pt. heavy cream
6 maraschino cherries

Soften gelatin in cold water, then heat very gently until gelatin is dissolved. Combine dissolved gelatin, nuts, sugar, and almond extract, and chill until mixture thickens. Whip cream until stiff and fold into gelatin mixture. Chill for at least 3 hours, then serve in sherbet glasses garnished with a maraschino cherry. Serves 6.

ORANGE CREAM

CREMA DI ARANCI

1 cup milk
⅓ cup sugar
½ teasp. cinnamon
Grated rind of 1 orange
1 jigger strega (orange liqueur); or, 1 jigger curacao
2 envelopes unflavored gelatin
¼ cup cold water
½ pt. heavy cream

Soak gelatin in cold water. Combine milk, sugar, cinnamon, orange rind, and strega, and cook slowly over hot, not boiling, water for 10 minutes, stirring constantly. Add softened gelatin, and stir until dissolved. Remove from stove, cool, and chill until mixture begins to thicken. Whip cream until stiff, and fold into gelatin mixture. Pour into 1 qt. mold or into 6 sherbet glasses, and chill at least 3 hours before serving. Serves 6. This cream makes an excellent filling and frosting for a cake. Spread just after folding in whipped cream, and store cake in refrigerator until serving time.
VARIATIONS: Other liqueurs which may be used instead of strega are apricot brandy, cherry brandy, sherry, or rum. Omit grated orange rind if rum is used.

MACAROON PUDDING

BUDINO DI AMARETTI

3 oz. (3 sqs.) unsweetened chocolate
3 cups milk
½ cup sugar
4 eggs, slightly beaten
½ cup macaroon crumbs

Combine chocolate and milk in a saucepan and heat over low flame until chocolate has melted. Beat with a rotary beater until well blended, and remove from heat. Beat eggs and sugar together until well blended, and then very slowly add eggs to hot chocolate mixture, stirring vigorously and constantly. Return pan to stove and cook until thick, stirring constantly, about 10 minutes. Turn off flame, add macaroon crumbs, and beat with rotary beater until smooth. Cool slightly, pour pudding into greased 1 qt. mold, and refrigerate. Chill at least 3 hours before serving. Serve topped with whipped cream. Enough for 4.

NUT PUDDING

BUDINO DI NOCE

3 eggs, separated
⅔ cup sugar
Grated rind of 1 orange
1 cup chopped almonds or hazelnuts
1 teasp. any liqueur
¼ cup macaroon crumbs

Beat egg yolks and sugar until light, add grated rind, nuts, and liqueur, and blend well. Beat egg whites until stiff, and fold them into yolk mixture. Pour into a 1 qt. greased mold, sprinkle with macaroon crumbs, and bake in a moderate oven 350° until set, about 25 minutes. Pudding should be soft, but not runny. Serve cold. Serves 4.
VARIATION: Chocolate Nut Pudding: Add 2 oz. (2 sqs.) unsweetened melted chocolate before folding in egg whites.

PISTACHIO DELIGHT

GATO DI PISTACCHIO

1 envelope unflavored gelatin
¼ cup cold water
1¼ cups milk
⅓ cup sugar
¼ cup chopped pistachio nuts
2 eggs, well beaten
1 tablesp. maraschino, or any desired liqueur
½ pt. heavy cream

Soften gelatin in cold water. Scald milk in top of double boiler, add gelatin, sugar, and nuts, and stir until gelatin and sugar are dissolved. Pour hot milk mixture over well beaten eggs, and return to double boiler. Cook over hot, not boiling, water until slightly thickened. Do not allow custard to boil. Remove from stove, and chill until thickened, but not set. Whip cream until stiff, and fold into thickened custard. Fold in maraschino, and pour into 1 qt. mold or into 6 sherbet glasses. Chill 3 hours before serving. Garnish with mint leaves. Serves 6.

RICE PUDDING

BUDINO DI RISO

½ cup uncooked rice	*½ cup raisins*
¼ cup sugar	*¼ teasp. nutmeg*
3 eggs	*¼ teasp. salt*
1 qt. milk	*1 tablesp. lemon juice*

1 teasp. grated lemon rind

Wash rice under cold running water until water is clear. Drain. Beat sugar and eggs together in greased baking dish, and add remaining ingredients and rice. Stir well, dot top with butter, and bake in moderate oven 350° until rice is tender and custard is set, about 35 minutes. Serve hot from baking dish with Brandied Cherry Sauce, see p. 205. Serves 6 to 8.

RUM GENOA DELIGHT

RUM GATO ALLA GENOVESE

1 cup macaroon crumbs (about 12 macaroons)	*¼ cup sugar*
	1 cup milk
¼ cup rum	*Grated rind of 1 orange*
1 envelope unflavored gelatin	*2 egg yolks, slightly beaten*

¼ teasp. almond extract

Combine macaroon crumbs and rum. Soften gelatin in cold milk. Add sugar and orange rind and cook over hot, not boiling, water until gelatin dissolves. Remove from stove and stir in beaten egg yolks gradually. Return to heat and simmer over hot, not boiling, water until custard coats spoon. Remove from stove, cool slightly, add flavoring, and fold in soaked crumbs. Pour mixture into 1 qt. mold, or into 6 sherbet glasses. Chill 3 hours before serving. Serve garnished with whipped cream and maraschino cherries, if desired. 6 servings.

TORTE NUT PUDDING: *See p. 258.*

TORTONI

6 egg yolks
Pinch of salt
3 tablesp. warm water
¾ cup sugar
¼ cup water
1 tablesp. vanilla
3 tablesp. sherry
1 pt. heavy cream
½ cup chopped almonds

Combine egg yolks, salt, and 3 tablesp. warm water in top of double boiler, and beat until yolks are light and lemon colored. Boil sugar and ¼ cup water over medium flame until syrup spins a thread from end of spoon, stirring constantly. Cool syrup slightly, and beat into egg yolks, beating rapidly and constantly. Cook over hot, not boiling, water until thick, stirring constantly, about 8 minutes. Remove from heat and cool to room temperature. Add vanilla and sherry. Let mixture cool further, and beat cream until thick but not stiff. Add cream to custard, stir, and pour into 12 fluted paper cups. Sprinkle tops with chopped almonds, and put cups in freezing compartment of refrigerator. Freeze until firm, about 3 hours. Serves 12. If desired, tortoni may be frozen in refrigerator tray, and served in sherbet glasses.

WHIPPED LIQUEUR

1 cup heavy cream
¼ cup confectioners sugar
1 egg white, stiffly beaten
3 tablesp. maraschino liqueur
Candied cherries; or, pieces of angelica

Whip cream until it will hold a slight peak. Gradually beat in sugar, then fold in stiffly beaten egg white and maraschino liqueur. Pack mixture into 12 small fluted paper cups, and top each cup with a candied cherry or angelica. Place cups in refrigerator tray and freeze without stirring until firm, 3 or 4 hours. Serve in same cups. Serves 12.
VARIATIONS: Other liqueurs may be used instead of maraschino. Use creme de menthe and garnish with candied mint leaves or sprigs of fresh mint. A green color may be obtained by adding 3 drops of green vegetable coloring to cream before whipping. Use rosolio, and garnish with candied rose petals. Use anisette and garnish with candied lemon peel. Or, use strega, and garnish with candied orange peel.

CLARET ICE

GRANITA DI VINO

2 lbs. Bing cherries
2 cups sugar
½ cup claret

Wash and pit cherries. Mash them with hands or potato masher until pulpy. Add sugar and wine, and let stand for 6 hours in a warm place. Strain and freeze in ice tray of refrigerator. Serves 4.

LEMON ICE

GRANITA DI LIMONE

4 cups water
1 cup sugar
Juice of 3 lemons
¼ cup cold water
1 envelope unflavored gelatin

Soften gelatin in ¼ cup cold water. Boil 4 cups water and sugar together 5 minutes. Remove from flame and add lemon juice. Add softened gelatin to syrup, and stir until dissolved. Place in ice tray of refrigerator and freeze until firm, about 3 hours. Serves 4.

ITALIAN SHERBET

GELATO

2 cups water
2 cups sugar
Pinch of salt
1 cup lemon juice
Grated rind of 1 lemon
2 egg whites

Boil water, sugar and salt together 5 minutes over medium flame. Strain lemon juice into sugar syrup and add grated lemon rind. Cool. Beat egg whites until stiff but not dry and fold them gently into cooled syrup. Pour into freezing tray of refrigerator, cover with waxed paper and freeze until firm, about 3 hours. Serves 6.

PEACH SHERBET

GELATO DI PESCHE

1 cup water
2 cups sugar
1 teasp. grated lemon rind
1 #2½ can peaches
Juice of 2 medium-sized oranges
½ teasp. rose water
½ teasp. almond extract
2 egg whites

Boil sugar, water, and lemon rind together 5 minutes. Remove from fire, and cool. Drain peaches, reserving 1 cup syrup. Rub peaches through sieve until you have 1 cup peach pulp. Add peach syrup, pulp, and orange juice to the cooled sugar syrup. Add rose water and almond flavoring. Blend well and pour into freezing tray of refrigerator. Cover with waxed paper and freeze until firm ½ in. in from side of tray. Scrape from freezing tray into chilled bowl and beat with chilled rotary beater until smooth but not melted. Fold in stiffly beaten egg whites, return immediately to tray, cover with waxed paper and return to refrigerator. Freeze until firm. Serves 6.

SPUMONI

I. BOTTOM LAYER

2 cups milk
1 cup sugar
4 egg yolks
¼ teasp. almond extract
1 tablesp. citron, chopped fine

Combine milk, sugar, egg yolks, and flavoring in saucepan, and cook slowly over low heat until thick. Cool and add citron. Freeze mixture in refrigerator tray until mushy, about 2 hours.

II. TOP LAYER

2 cups milk
2 tablesp. cornstarch
¾ cup sugar
1 cup heavy cream
1 tablesp. chopped almonds
2 drops green food coloring

Combine milk, cornstarch, and sugar, and stir until dissolved. Cook over low flame until thick. Cool. Whip cream until stiff, and fold into cooled custard. Add nuts and coloring, and blend. Freeze in refrigerator tray until mushy, about 2 hours.

III. CENTER LAYER

2 cups heavy cream
½ cup confectioners sugar
2 tablesp. rum
¼ cup cocoa

Whip cream until stiff and fold in other ingredients.

Prepare mixtures in order given. When first two have become mushy, prepare the third. Chill 2 large bombe molds. Put bottom layer in with spoon; spread it evenly with a spatula over inside of molds to ½ in. thickness. Then spoon in third, whipped-cream mixture until mold is almost filled. Cover with second mixture. Place a piece of waxed paper over molds, cover, and freeze in freezing compartment of refrigerator for about 2 hours, until very solid. Cut in wedges to serve. Enough for 8 to 10 people.

WINE FLUFF

VINO BORRA

2 eggs | *1 teasp. sugar*
¼ cup marsala or sherry

Beat eggs in top of cold double boiler 5 minutes. Add sugar gradually, continuing to beat until sugar is completely dissolved. Add marsala and beat until well blended. Cook over just-boiling water, beating constantly, until mixture begins to thicken. Make sure that water does not touch top part of double boiler. Do not overcook. Remove from fire, pour into large serving dish or sherbet cups, and chill. Serves 2. This custard may also be served immediately as a hot dessert. Or, it may be used as a cake filling when chilled.

ZABAGLIONE

4 egg yolks | *¾ cup port or marsala*
4 tablesp. sugar | *Pinch of cinnamon*

Beat yolks until they are light and lemon colored. Gradually add sugar, beating constantly. Add wine, and beat thoroughly. Place these ingredients in top of double boiler and cook over hot, but not boiling, water until thick, beating continuously with rotary beater. Pour immediately in dessert dishes, sprinkle with cinnamon, and serve. Or, chill, and serve as a sauce over fruit. Serves 6.

CHAPTER SEVENTEEN

Fruits and Nuts

MAMA MIA ALMOND PASTE

PASTA DI MANDORLA

½ lb. shelled almonds
2 egg whites
1½ cups sifted confectioners sugar
1 teasp. lemon juice
3 drops almond oil; or, ½ teasp. almond extract, rose water, or any other flavoring

Blanch almonds and put them through food chopper 3 times, using finest blade. Beat egg whites until stiff but not dry. Stir in sugar, lemon juice, and flavoring. Knead gently into a smooth paste, adding more sugar if necessary. Paste must be very smooth. Store paste in covered airtight container or jar and let stand in refrigerator 4 or 5 days before using. This paste is excellent for almond sauce; for cookies, cake fillings, and frostings; and for marzipan.

UNCOOKED MARZIPAN

MARZAPANE NON COTTO

1 lb. shelled almonds
2 cups sifted confectioners sugar
1¼ cups granulated sugar
½ teasp. almond extract
2 egg whites, beaten stiff

Blanch almonds and put them through food chopper 3 times, using finest blade. Combine with remaining ingredients, and knead until smooth and creamy, adding additional sugar if necessary. If paste becomes too stiff, add a few drops of lemon juice. Cover with a damp cloth and store in refrigerator overnight before using. Then, tint with diluted vegetable colorings and shape into vegetables and fruits. Or use the marzipan to stuff figs or pitted dates.

BAKED APPLES

COTTURA AL FORNO

4 baking apples
4 teasp. sugar
¼ cup raisins; or
¼ cup semi-sweet chocolate bits
¼ teasp. grated lemon rind
1 cup marsala or white wine

Wash apples, core, and peel off ½ in. strip around the stem end. Put in a baking dish pared end up, and fill cavity with 1 teasp. sugar, and a few raisins or chocolate bits. Sprinkle each apple with a pinch of grated lemon rind, and pour wine over all. Bake in a moderate oven 375° until soft, about 45 minutes, basting frequently with wine. Serve hot or cold. Serves 4. These apples make an excellent side dish with pork; or, they may be used alone as a dessert.

BRANDIED CHERRIES

CILIEGIE AL LIQUORE

2 lbs. Bing cherries
2 cups brandy
1 cup water
2 cups sugar

Wash cherries and cut off half the stems. Place in jar, and cover with brandy. Cover jars, but do not seal. Let stand over-

night. Boil sugar and water together 10 minutes. Skim surface, and cool. Drain brandy from cherries, and add to syrup. Stir well, and pour liquid back into jar over cherries. Seal. Let stand 1 month before using. Makes 2 qts.
VARIATION: Brandied Figs: Use 12 fresh Italian figs instead of cherries.

BRANDY CHERRY SAUCE: *See p. 205.*

BRANDY PEACHES

PESCHE AL LIQUORE

2 lbs. peaches | *2 cups water*
3½ cups sugar | *½ in. piece stick cinnamon*
1 cup brandy

Plunge peaches into boiling water 1 minute. Peel. Boil sugar, water, and cinnamon stick 5 minutes. Skim surface. Add peeled peaches and cook until tender, about 5 minutes. Test with toothpick. Remove peaches from hot syrup with slotted spoon, and place in hot sterilized jars. Add brandy to syrup in pan, bring to a boil, and pour over hot fruit. Seal tightly. Let stand 1 month before using. Makes 2 qts.
VARIATIONS: Brandy Apricots: Use 2 lbs. fresh apricots instead of peaches.
Brandy Pears: Use 2 lbs. Seckel pears instead of peaches.

CHESTNUTS

CASTAGNE

Chestnuts must be blanched and shelled before they can be used. There are 3 ways to blanch them:

1. Make a cross-shaped gash with a sharp knife on the flat side of each chestnut; or, make ½ in. slit on each side of the

nut. Put in a deep saucepan or frying pan with ¼ cup of salad oil for each lb. of chestnuts. Cover and cook over low heat 10 minutes until skins have loosened. Shake pan while nuts are cooking. Remove from stove, and when nuts are cool enough to handle, remove shells and skins. This is the quickest way.

2. Cut slits in each chestnut and place in a shallow pan with 3 tablesp. oil for each lb. of nuts. Bake in very hot oven 450° 15 minutes until chestnuts start popping. Wait a few minutes before taking them out of the oven until they have finished popping, because you may easily get burnt otherwise. Remove shells and skins when cool enough to handle.

3. Cut slits in each nut, and put in a pan with water to cover. Boil gently until tender, about 30 minutes. Drain, and remove shells and skins. Chestnuts prepared this way are easily pureed or mashed.

Dried chestnuts, which may be purchased at an Italian grocery store, are already shelled and blanched. To prepare them for use, cover them with cold water and let stand overnight. These nuts are not as tasty as the freshly shelled nuts.

BRANDY CHESTNUTS

CASTAGNE AL LIQUORE

1 lb. chestnuts, blanched and shelled
1 cup water
1¼ cups sugar
1 cup brandy

Boil sugar and water together 10 minutes. Skim surface. Put peeled chestnuts in a bowl, and pour the hot syrup over them. Cover and let stand overnight. Next day, drain syrup from chestnuts and combine with brandy in a saucepan. Bring to a boil. Put chestnuts in hot, sterilized jars, and pour boiling syrup over them. Seal tightly. Let stand 1 month before using. Makes 1 qt.

STEAMED CHOCOLATE CHESTNUT PUDDING

BUDINO DI CASTAGNE E CIOCCOLATA

1 lb. chestnuts, pureed
¼ cup cocoa
2 cups milk
¼ cup sugar
2 teasp. butter
1 egg
1 tablesp. rum, curacao, or sherry
½ teasp. vanilla

Combine cocoa, milk, sugar and butter, and cook slowly over hot water 10 minutes, stirring constantly. Add pureed chestnuts and egg, and stir well. Butter a 1-qt. mold and pour mixture into it. Place in a pan of hot water, and bake in a moderate oven 350° until pudding is firm, about 45 minutes. Serve immediately. Serves 6.

CRYSTALLIZED CHESTNUTS

CRISTALLIZZARE CASTAGNE

1 lb. chestnuts, blanched and shelled
1 cup sugar
½ cup water
1 2-in. piece stick cinnamon
1½ tablesp. rum or brandy

Boil sugar, water, and cinnamon without stirring until a drop forms a soft ball in cold water. Skim surface, cool, and add rum and chestnuts. Stir mixture gently with wooden spoon until it becomes creamy. Pour on a greased platter, and separate chestnuts with a spoon. Serves 5 or 6.

MERINGUED CHESTNUTS

CASTAGNE MIRINGHE

1 lb. chestnuts, blanched and shelled
2 egg whites
2 cups confectioners sugar
1 teasp. cinnamon

Cut peeled chestnuts in half lengthwise. Beat egg whites slightly until foamy. Mix sugar and cinnamon. Dip chestnuts in egg whites, then roll in sugar and cinnamon. Place a sheet of heavy brown paper on a cookie sheet or oven rack. Grease the paper liberally, and arrange the chestnuts on it. Bake in moderate oven 350° 10 minutes, until golden brown. Serves 6. VARIATIONS: Use 1 lb. pulled figs in place of chestnuts. Do not cook figs. Or, use 1 lb. of some other kind of shelled nuts, such as almonds or pecans.

CHESTNUT SOUFFLÉ

SUFFLE DI CASTAGNE

1 lb. chestnuts, blanched and peeled
2 cups milk
¼ teasp. salt
½ cup sugar
¼ tablesp. melted butter
2 tablesp. maraschino liqueur
½ teasp. vanilla
6 eggs, separated

Place peeled chestnuts in saucepan with milk, add salt, and cover. Cook slowly over low flame until soft, about 30 minutes. Drain, and mash with a fork, then rub through a sieve. Mix puree with sugar, butter, maraschino, and vanilla. Blend well. Beat egg yolks until thick and lemon colored, and fold into chestnut mixture. Beat egg whites until stiff but not dry, and fold into chestnut mixture. Pour into ungreased 1½ qt. casserole and bake in moderate oven 350° until knife inserted in center of soufflé comes out clean, about 30 minutes. Sprinkle top with powdered sugar if desired, and serve immediately as dessert. Serves 6.

CHESTNUT TORTE

TORTE DI CASTAGNE

¾ cup chestnut puree (1 lb. chestnuts)
1 cup cake flour
1 teasp. baking powder
6 tablesp. butter
⅔ cup sugar
1 teasp. vanilla
6 eggs, separated

Sift flour, measure, and resift with baking powder 3 times. Cream butter and sugar, add chestnut puree and vanilla, and beat well. Add egg yolks one at a time and beat well after each addition. Beat egg whites until they hold a soft peak. Fold whites into chestnut mixture. Fold sifted dry ingredients into mixture. Line a greased oblong 9 by 13 in. pan with waxed paper, and bake torte in this pan in moderate oven 350° 40 minutes, or until cake shrinks from side of pan. Cool in pan for 5 minutes, then turn out on cake rack and remove waxed paper. Cool. If desired, sprinkle top with confectioners sugar. Serves 8 to 10. This torte will keep very well if wrapped in waxed paper and stored in a cool dry place.

CHRISTMAS FRUIT BALLS

1 cup pulled figs
1 cup dried apricots
½ cup candied orange peel
½ cup candied cherries
1 cup toasted almonds
¼ cup honey
1 teasp. lemon or orange juice
1 cup sifted confectioners sugar

Wash figs and apricots, and put them through food chopper with orange peel, cherries, and nuts, using medium blade. Work in honey and fruit juice, using enough liquid so that mixture holds together. Take heaping teaspoonfuls of mixture and shape into balls between palms of hands. Roll balls in confectioners sugar. When they harden, wrap them in waxed paper and store them in airtight container. Makes 2 dozen small balls.

FRUIT CONSERVE

CONSERVA DI FRUTTA

Fifth of brandy
1 lb. small white seedless grapes; 1 lb. sugar
1 pt. strawberries, washed and hulled; ½ cup sugar
½ lb. cherries, pitted; ½ cup sugar
3 plums, halved and pitted; 3 tablesp. sugar
2 peaches, peeled, halved, and pitted; ¼ cup sugar
6 apricots, pitted; ¼ cup sugar

Place fruits in order given in a large wide-mouthed crock or gallon jar. Use sugar in amounts given to cover each fruit. Repeat layers until all ingredients are used. Pour brandy into crock, and seal. Let stand 1 month. Serve fruit with liquid from jar.

FRUIT AND NUT GLACÉ

2⅓ cups sugar
½ cup water
Pinch of cream of tartar

Combine ingredients in saucepan and cook over low flame, stirring constantly until sugar is dissolved. Cover and bring to the boiling point; boil without stirring until a drop of syrup snaps easily under cold water. Remove from fire and pour over fruits or nuts immediately. Sufficient glacé to cover 1 lb. fruit or nuts.

FIG BALLS

DOLCE ALLA FICI

½ lb. Italian figs
¼ cup toasted almonds or other nuts
Rind of ½ orange
1 teasp. vanilla
2 tablesp. orange or lemon juice

Wash figs and put them in a colander over a pot of hot water. Cover colander and steam figs over medium flame 10 minutes. Remove and cool. Grind figs with almonds and orange peel, using medium blade. Add vanilla and orange juice to ground figs, and mix thoroughly. If mixture is too firm to handle easily, add a little more orange juice or lemon juice. Take heaping teaspoonfuls of mixture and form into balls with palms of hands. Roll in granulated sugar. 2 dozen small balls.

FIG SAUCE: *See p. 206.*

STUFFED FIGS

FICI IMBOTTITI

1 dozen pulled figs
2 egg whites
1 lb. sifted confectioners sugar
1 teasp. anise or almond extract; or, sherry, lemon juice, or orange juice

Remove stem end of figs and split open lengthwise. Beat egg whites until stiff but not dry. Gradually beat in confectioners sugar. Blend in desired flavoring, and stuff cavity in figs with mixture. Roll in additional confectioners sugar if desired.
VARIATION: 12 to 15 large dates may be used instead of figs. Roll in granulated sugar.

FRUIT FRITTERS

FRITELLE DI FRUTTA

4 medium-sized oranges
2 tablesp. confectioners sugar
¼ cup any desired liqueur or rum

Peel oranges and cut into sections. Sprinkle with sugar and pour liqueur over them. Allow to stand for 2 hours, then drain. Dip sections in the following batter:

2 eggs, separated
¼ cup milk
1 teasp. oil or melted butter
½ teasp. salt
2 teasp. baking powder
1 cup sifted flour

Beat egg yolks until thick and lemon colored. Add milk and melted butter and mix well. Sift dry ingredients together and beat into yolk mixture until batter is smooth. Beat egg whites until stiff and fold into yolks.

Dip orange sections in this batter and fry in deep hot fat 365° until they are light brown and puffy, about 3 minutes. Drain on absorbent paper and sprinkle with confectioners sugar. About 2 dozen.

APPLE FRITTERS

FRITTELLE DI MELA

6 tart apples
2 tablesp. lemon juice
2 tablesp. sugar
1 teasp. cinnamon

Pare and slice apples into ¼ in. slices. Sprinkle with lemon juice, sugar and cinnamon and let stand for 1 hour. Drain. Dip in batter and fry as directed. Roll in granulated sugar. Makes 2 dozen.

VARIATIONS:

APRICOT FRITTERS: Substitute 1½ dozen apricots, quartered, for apples.

BANANA FRITTERS: Substitute 5 medium-size bananas cut in 2 in. pieces for apples. Add 1 jigger of rum to lemon juice. Makes 2 dozen.

CHERRY FRITTERS: Substitute 2 lbs. fresh pitted cherries for apples. Makes 2 dozen.

STUFFED PEACHES

PESCHE IMBOTTITE

6 large fresh peaches
¼ cup macaroon or lady finger crumbs
½ cup finely ground almonds
1 teasp. grated orange rind
2 tablesp. confectioners sugar
½ cup sherry

Wash, peel, halve, and pit peaches. Place cut side up in baking dish. Combine crumbs, almonds and orange rind and fill peach cavities with this mixture. Sprinkle with confectioners sugar, and pour sherry over all. Ten minutes before serving time, place peaches in oven and bake at moderate temperature 375° for 10 minutes. Serve immediately. Serves 6.

PEACHES WITH WINE CREAM

PESCHE CON CREMA VINO

3 large firm peaches
3 egg yolks
3 tablesp. sugar
6 tablesp. sherry or marsala

Wash, peel, halve, and pit peaches. Combine egg yolks and sugar in top of cold double boiler and beat until creamy and lemon colored. Add wine gradually, beating constantly. Cook over hot, never boiling, water, beating continuously, until thick, about 5 minutes. Put peaches in serving dishes, pour hot wine sauce over them, and serve immediately. Or, chill both peaches and wine sauce, and serve cold. Serves 6.

PEARS WITH WINE

PERE CON VINO

2 firm pears
½ cup sugar
½ cup water
1 stick cinnamon
½ cup Italian red wine
1 recipe Zabaglione, *see p. 244*
(omit cinnamon)
4 maraschino cherries

Peel pears, halve, and core. Boil sugar and water until syrupy, about 10 minutes, stirring until sugar is dissolved. Add pears, cinnamon stick, and wine to syrup, and simmer until pears are tender but not mushy, about 20 minutes. Chill pears in syrup 1 hour. Place half a pear in sherbet glass and spoon 1 tablesp. of pear syrup over it. Top with zabaglione, and garnish with cherry. Serves 4.

VARIATION: If desired, the pears may be served with cake instead of zabaglione. Slice sponge cake 1 in. thick, and place pear on cake. Pour pear syrup over both, and serve immediately.

STRAWBERRIES WITH WINE

FRAGOLE CON VINO

1 qt. fresh strawberries
½ cup marsala or sauterne
2 tablesp. sugar (optional)

Wash, hull, and chill strawberries. Chill wine, and pour over berries. Sprinkle with sugar if desired, and serve at once. Serves 6.

STRAWBERRY ICE

GRANITA DI FRAGOLE

1 qt. strawberries
Juice of ½ lemon
Grated rind of ½ lemon
2 cups water
2 cups sugar

Wash and hull strawberries, and crush to a pulp with hands or potato masher. Add lemon rind and lemon juice, and let stand 15 minutes. Boil sugar and water together 10 minutes, remove from flame, and add to crushed strawberries. Stir well, cool, and strain. Fill a tall glass with crushed ice, and pour in ¼ cup strawberry syrup. Stir well, and add more water if desired. Serve with cookies. Serves 6 to 8.

TORTE NUT PUDDING

BUDINO TORTA DI NOCCIOLE

4 egg yolks
¾ cup sugar
¼ teasp. salt
2 cups milk
2 oz. (2 sqs.) unsweetened chocolate
1 jigger dark rum or creme de menthe
1 cup chopped pistachio nuts

Beat egg yolks slightly, and add sugar and salt. Heat milk and chocolate together until chocolate melts and milk just begins to boil. Beat with wire whisk until well blended. Stir in nuts and rum. Add chocolate mixture to egg yolks, blend well, and pour into 1 qt. baking dish. Bake in moderate oven 350° 30 minutes, until a silver knife inserted into center will come out clean. Chill, and serve in sherbet glasses. Serves 6.

CHAPTER EIGHTEEN

Beverages

AFTER DINNER COFFEE

CAFFE ESPRESSO

To make coffee the Italian way, a *caffetiera,* a device similar to a drip coffee pot, is necessary. Use 3 tablesp. pulverized Italian coffee for 2 cups of water. Put the coffee in the middle compartment of the pot. Pour the cold water into the lower compartment, and cover the pot with the top compartment. Put the pot over a high flame until steam comes from the small hole. Remove the pot from the fire, holding both handles tightly, and reverse the entire coffee maker, so that the top compartment is on the bottom. Let the hot water drip through the coffee, and as soon as it has all gone through, serve the coffee in demitasse cups. You may like to serve a twist of lemon peel in the coffee, or a jigger of cherry liqueur. Or, serve sugar with it as a regular demitasse.

ITALIAN WINES

The flavor of good Italian food is considerably enhanced when it is accompanied by good Italian wine. Italians consider wine a food, which it is; and it is very seldom indeed that an Italian meal is placed on the table without some kind of wine being served with it. Sweet or dry vermouth, with a twist of lemon peel and a dash of bitters, is drunk as an aperitif. A dry red wine is usually served with a meat meal, and a dry white wine with antipasto, soups, pastas made without meat, fish, or poultry. Dessert wines are served with the cheeses, fruits, and pastries which end the dinner. On an especially festive occasion a sparkling wine may be drunk with dessert. After-dinner liqueurs are also consumed as part of the meal.

Wines are produced in every section of the Italian countryside, from Piedmont in the north to the islands of Sicily and Sardinia in the south. The remarkable variety and number of Italian wines reflect the widely different conditions under which they are grown, and it would not be too much to say that almost any kind of wine you might wish to drink is made someplace in Italy.

Some excellent Italian wines are imported into this country at a reasonable price, many no more expensive than our own fine domestic products. Italian wines are produced and bottled under strict government supervision, and their origin and sound quality are guaranteed by the National Institute for Foreign Trade (*Istituto Nazionale per il Commercio Estero*), whose stamp appears on every inspected bottle. You may easily and safely become acquainted with most of the types of wine that Italy exports, and a little experimentation will soon indicate which wines best meet the requirements of your own taste.

The Italian wines most widely distributed in America are these:

RED WINES:

Barolo: A dry, ruby-red, full-bodied wine, with a smooth velvety taste. It is produced in Piedmont.

Barbera: A delicate dry or semi-sweet wine, whose bouquet improves with age. Also produced in Piedmont.

Bardolino: A clear, light, ruddy wine, with a pleasingly dry taste. It should be drunk while still young. Made in Venetia.

Valpolicella: An excellent, deep ruby-colored wine, with a delicate bouquet and mellow taste. Wonderful with any kind of meat dish. A Venetian wine.

Chianti: Probably the best known of Italian reds, this Tuscan wine has a slightly prickly taste when young, which disappears as the wine ages.

Brolio: Very much like Chianti, it is grown in the same neighborhood in Tuscany. Like Chianti, also, it improves with age.

Ciro di Calabria: A deep, ruby-red wine, which should be allowed to mature to develop its full flavor.

Faro: A Sicilian wine of a bright ruby color, with an excellent bouquet and flavor.

WHITE WINES:

Valtellina: A light, straw-colored wine with a fresh taste. Made in Lombardy.

Terlano: A choice white wine from the Upper Audige, beautifully translucent, with an elegant bouquet.

Soave: A soft, velvety, dry wine, made from grapes grown near Verona.

Orvieto: The best-known, and one of the choicest of Italian white wines. There are 2 types, one dry and the other fruity. Both varieties have an attractive light-yellow color and an exquisitely delicate bouquet. From Umbria.

Frascati: A limpid, golden-yellow wine, with a mellow flavor. It also is made in 2 types, dry and fruity. A wine of historic Latium.

Est-est-est Montefiascone: A golden wine produced near the Lake of Bolsena. Made in 2 types, dry and sweet. One of the most famous wines of Italy.

Lacrima Christi del Vesuvio: A straw-colored wine, sweet, velvety, and aromatic. The grapes are grown in vineyards on the southern slopes of Mount Vesuvius.

Sansevero: A fine, clear, delicate wine, excellent with fish. One of the best wines of the Apulian district.

Vernaccia del Campidano: A dry, amber-colored wine, with a bouquet reminiscent of almond blossoms, and pleasingly bitter. A wine of Sardinia.

DESSERT WINES:

Flore della Alpi: A sweet, potent liqueur, made with cinnamon sticks and rock sugar. A product of Piedmont.

Vin Santo: Golden-yellow, sweet, smooth wine of Tuscany.

Aleatico di Puglia: A red Apulian liqueur wine, with a strong aroma, full taste, and pleasant, sweet flavor.

Moscato di Salento: Another Apulian dessert wine, with a warm, generous, subtle bouquet.

Greco di Gerace: A delicate, smooth, golden-yellow dessert wine from Calabria, whose bouquet will remind you of orange blossoms. This choice wine is produced in limited quantities.

Marsala: The best known of Italian dessert wines. Produced in Sicily in 2 types, dry and sweet. It is a limpid, brilliant wine with a fine full flavor. Excellent for cooking as well as for drinking.

Nasco: A generous, brilliant, golden-yellow dessert wine from Sardinia, with a delicate flavor heightened by faint undertones of bitterness.

SPARKLING WINES:

Asti spumante: The standard for all Italian sparkling wines, made in Piedmont. Very delicate bouquet, and a fresh, sweet taste.

Prosecco de Conegliano: A brilliant, sparkling white wine made in Venetia. It must be drunk young. It has a distinguished bouquet and a flavor underscored by a very slight trace of bitterness.

Moscato and *Lacrima Christi del Vesuvio* are also produced as sparkling wines.

LIQUEURS

LIQUORE

Liqueurs, or cordials, are highly flavored, sweetened wines served as after-dinner drinks. They are ordinarily served at room temperature in very small liqueur glasses, for a little of them goes a long way. Italians feel that a liqueur after a heavy meal aids the digestion. Whether it does or not, the custom of sitting with friends, talking quietly, and sipping a fragrant *liquore* is without doubt a pleasantly relaxing way to end a good dinner.

Here are some of the characteristic Italian liqueurs, with suggestions for their use in cooking:

Anisette: Colorless, with an anise flavor. Use it to flavor icings and cookies. Sometimes added to highballs, pickles, frappés, and flips.

Caffe Sport: Coffee colored and coffee flavored. Use it in icings and as a sauce over ice cream and puddings.

Creme de menthe: Green or white, with a peppermint flavor. Use it in sour mixed drinks, frappés, cocktails and icings, or as a sauce for ice cream and puddings.

Grappa: Grape flavored, with a brandy base.

Maraschino: Red, cherry flavored liqueur. Use it in icings, soufflés, and sour drinks.

Strega: Yellow, with an orange flavor. May be added to caffe espresso, or used in aromatic drinks, icings, and cake fillings.

Rosolio: Ruby colored, with a very sweet rose flavor. Made from the petals of fresh roses. Use it to flavor sour drinks, cake fillings, icings, and as a sauce over ice cream. And try a very little of it in iced tea.

All these cordials can be bought in most liquor stores, although many Italian homemakers still follow the tradition of preparing their own *liquore*. Liqueurs are a part of many Italian family celebrations. At a wedding, for instance, it is customary for the groom to offer guests a glass of liqueur, and for the guests in return to offer a toast to the bride and groom.

CHAMPAGNE PUNCH

PONCE DI SCIAMPAGNA

4 fluid oz. maraschino liqueur
2 fluid oz. curacao
1 8-oz. jar maraschino cherries
2 sprigs fresh mint (optional)
1 28-oz. bottle carbonated water
1 26-oz. bottle champagne

Put maraschino liqueur, curacao, and maraschino cherries with their liquid into bowl or jar. Cover tightly and refrigerate for 4 hours. Chill unopened carbonated water and champagne. Chill punch bowl and rub with mint. Pour maraschino mixture into chilled punch bowl and stir thoroughly. Just before serving, add chilled carbonated water and champagne. Serve in chilled cups or glasses. Serves 12.

ROMAN PUNCH

PONCE ROMANA

2 cups sugar
1 cup water
Rind of ½ lemon
Rind of ½ orange
Juice of 3 lemons
Juice of 3 oranges
¼ cup brandy
2 tablesp. rum
1 26-oz. bottle chilled champagne

Boil sugar and water in saucepan over low flame 10 minutes. Skim, and remove from stove. Add fruit rinds and juices, and cool to room temperature. Stir well, put in large jar, and chill in refrigerator 4 hours. Chill champagne and punch bowl, also. Strain syrup mixture through coarse mesh strainer into punch bowl. Add brandy, rum, and chilled champagne. Mix thoroughly, garnish with mint leaves or lemon slices, and serve in chilled punch cups. Serves 12.

RUM OR BRANDY PUNCH

PONCE DI RUM

2 cups sugar
1 cup water
Juice of 5 or 6 oranges
Juice of 4 lemons
Fifth of light rum or brandy
2 oz. grenadine (optional)
1 bottle carbonated water
Orange slices

Boil sugar and water in saucepan over low flame 10 minutes. Skim top, cool slightly and add fruit juices. Stir well and chill. Chill punch bowl also. Put syrup mixture through coarse mesh strainer, and pour into punch bowl. Add rum and grenadine and stir well. Add 1 tray ice cubes, and carbonated water. Stir gently, garnish with orange slices, and serve in chilled punch cups. Serves 12.

HOT WINE PUNCH

PONCE DI VINO

Fifth of Italian red wine; claret, or burgundy
1 2-in. piece stick cinnamon; or, ¼ teasp. ground cloves
Rind of 1 lemon
Rind of 1 orange
½ cup sugar

Pour wine in stainless steel or enamel pan (not aluminum) and add cinnamon stick, lemon rind, orange rind, and sugar. Bring to a boil, reduce heat, and boil 1 minute. Remove from stove, and serve immediately in mugs or cups. Serves 10 to 12.

CHAPTER NINETEEN

Glossary of Italian Cooking Terms

Acciughe	Anchovy
Aceto	Vinegar
Affogato	Smothered
Aglio	Garlic
Agnello	Lamb
Albicocca	Apricot
Alla	In the style of
Amaretti	Macaroons
Animella	Sweetbreads
Anguilla	Eel
Anice	Anise
Anitra	Duck
Antipasto	Appetizers
Aragosta	Lobster
Arancia	Orange
Arancini	Patties
Arnione	Kidneys
Arrostiti	Roasted
Avellane	Filberts
Baccala	Dried codfish
Bardana	Burdock
Biscotti	Cookies; biscuits

Bistecca	Beefsteak
Bollito	Boiled
Borra	Fluff
Braciuolini	Beef rolls
Brodo	Broth
Budino	Pudding
Bue	Beef
Cacciatora	Hunter style
Caffe	Coffee
Caffetiera	Italian coffee pot
Calamai	Squid
Cannella	Cinnamon
Cannoli	Fried hollow pastries
Capocollo	Italian smoked pork
Capitone	A kind of large eel
Cappelletti	Little hats; filled pasta
Carciofi	Artichokes
Carne	Meat
Cassata Siciliana	Rich cream cake
Castagna	Chestnut
Cavolfiore	Cauliflower
Cavolo	Cabbage
Cavolrapa	Kohlrabi
Ceci	Chick peas
Cervelli	Brains
Cervo	Venison
Chiocciola	Snail
Cicoria	Dandelion
Ciliege	Cherry
Cioccolata	Chocolate
Cipolla	Onion
Con	With
Conchiglia	Scallops
Condimento	Salad dressing
Coniglio	Rabbit

Costatelle	Chops
Costole	Spareribs
Cotoletta	Veal cutlet
Cotto	Cooked
Crema	Cream
Croche	Croquettes
Crostini	Toasted bread squares
Cucidata	Filled cookies
Cuscinetti	Small fried sandwiches
Dolce	Sweet
Dolce e agro	Sweet and sour
E	And
Escarola	Escarole
Fagiano	Pheasant
Fagioli	Beans
Fagiolini	String beans
Farfallette	Fried pastry strips
Fava	Green lima-like beans
Fegato	Liver
Fico	Fig
Finocchio	Fennel
Formaggio	Cheese
Forno	Baked
Fragole	Strawberries
Frittata	Omelet
Fritto	Fried
Fritto misto	Mixed fry
Frollo	Soft
Frusta	Whipped
Funghi	Mushrooms
Gamberi	Shrimp
Gato	Cake

Gelato	Italian sherbet
Ghiacciata	Cake frosting
Gnocchi	Dumplings
Granchi	Crabs
Granita	Italian ice
Griglia	Grilled
Guastelle	Sicilian rolls
Imbottite	Stuffed
Insalata	Salad
Lasagne	Noodles
Lenticchi	Lentils
Lettuga	Lettuce
Limatura	Cake filling
Limone	Lemon
Lingua	Tongue
Liquore	Liqueur
Maiale	Pork
Mandorla	Almond
Manzo	Beef
Marinara	Mariner style
Marinate	Marinade
Marsala	Heavy, semi-sweet dessert sherry
Melenzana	Eggplant
Menta	Mint
Merluzzo	Whiting
Miele	Honey
Milanese	Milan style
Minestra	Soup
Minestrone	Thick vegetable soup
Miringhe	Meringue
Mitili	Mussels
Mozzarella	Fresh unsalted cheese

Napoletana	Neapolitan style
Nero	Black
Ostriche	Oysters
Pan di Spagne	Sponge cake
Pane	Bread
Parmesan	Grating cheese
Parmigiana	Made with Parmesan
Pasta	Paste; dough
Pastini	Small cookies
Patate	Potatoes
Peperoni	Peppers
Pere	Pears
Pesce	Fish
Pesce Spada	Swordfish
Pesche	Peaches
Pernici	Partridges
Piccante	Piquant
Piccione	Squab
Pignoli	Pine nuts
Piselli	Peas
Pizza	Pie
Polenta	Cornmeal
Pollo	Chicken; fowl
Polpette	Meat balls
Polpo	Octopus
Pomodoro	Tomato
Ponce	Punch
Prosciutto	Italian ham
Provolone	Cured cheese
Quaglia	Quail
Ranocchie	Frogs legs
Ravioli	Stuffed pasta

Ricetta	Recipe
Ricotta	Italian cottage cheese
Ripieno	Stuffed; filling
Riso	Rice
Romano	Grating cheese
Salsa	Sauce
Salsiccia	Sausage
Sarde	Sardines
Savoiardi	Lady fingers
Scaloppini	Veal sliced paper-thin
Scungilli	Conch
Semplice	Simple
Senza	Without
Sfingi	Small cakes; puffs
Sfogliata	Pie dough
Siciliana	Sicilian style
Sparagio	Asparagus
Spinaci	Spinach
Spumoni	Italian ice cream
Stiacciata	Muffins
Strufoli	Clusters
Suffle	Soufflé
Tacchino	Turkey
Tagliarini	Narrow noodles
Tartufata	Truffles
Tonno	Tuna
Torta	Pie; torte
Trippa	Tripe
Trota	Trout
Umido	Stew
Uovo	Egg

Verde	Green
Vino	Wine
Vitello	Veal
Vongoli	Clams
Zabaglione	Wine custard
Zucchero	Sugar
Zucchini	Italian squash
Zuppa	Soup

Index